ASK AT DESK FOR ACCOMPANYING GLASSES.

the intelligent eye

Weidenfeld & Nicolson 5 Winsley Street London W1

Designed by Peter Wildbur
for George Weidenfeld and Nicolson Ltd

ISBN 0 297 00476 X

Printed by Jarrold and Sons Ltd, Norwich

Contents

Foreword

This book has its origin in the Royal Institution Christmas Lectures of 1967–8, which I was privileged to deliver. The Christmas Lectures have been presented without a break, apart from the Second World War, since 1826. Previous lecturers have been distinguished indeed, including Michael Faraday who gave the lectures on nineteen occasions between 1827 and 1860, establishing the tradition of illustrating them with a large number of demonstrations and experiments. Among lecturers since have been Sir William Bragg, Sir James Jeans and many other distinguished scientists, including Professor Sir Frederic Bartlett, lately Professor of Experimental Psychology at Cambridge, who was my teacher.

My immediate predecessor was Professor Eric Laithwaite, whose lectures 'The Engineer in Wonderland' were for the first time televised on BBC 2. Mine were also televised, for the first time in colour. I am grateful to the producer, Alan Sleath, for the time and care he devoted to their presentation, and for arranging for the resources of the BBC which were given most generously. Philip Daly's 'backroom' advice I much appreciate – in fact the presentation of one of the lectures was changed at the last moment on his suggestion. Colin Haycraft has given help over transforming the lectures into book form, and so has John Curtis in seeing it through the press and giving invaluable advice at all stages.

For building the demonstrations and drawing the figures, I owe a great debt to many people including my colleagues: Dr Jim Howe, Steven Salter, Roly Lishman, Stephen Young, Tony Downing, Ian Low, Don Cox, Philip Clark and my wife, Frëja. Christopher Marshall drew the line illustrations. Outstanding for their support and advice were 'Bill' Coates, Senior Experimental Officer of the RI, and his staff. As all who have given discourses at the RI know, Bill is truly a genius at averting disaster and has an answer to every problem.

The Director of the Royal Institution, Professor George Porter, sacrificed his time to be present at every rehearsal and smoothed out many difficulties. I am most grateful to him and his wife for their kindness and help.

The six lectures covered a wide field, the topics being chosen to maintain the interest of both a live and a television audience covering a large age range – I suppose from fourteen to eighty – with an emphasis on the young. This book is not intended as a record of the lectures – it is rather an essay on their title. The lectures were built round a great number of demonstrations, including conjuring tricks arranged by Alan Sleath, which cannot be presented in book form. Also, some of the material is already available in my book *Eye and Brain* (World University Library, 1966) and I am anxious not to repeat the same material under the guise of a different title. There is no doubt that giving a course of lectures is the best way of developing one's ideas: I hope that in this book I succeed in passing on some of the benefit that I derived from giving the Christmas Lectures.

R.L.G.

Acknowledgements

The majority of the photographs in this book were taken by the author with Philip Clark.

The following illustrations were specially drawn by Christopher Marshall: 4, 5, 6, 7, 8, 9, 10, 19, 21, 23, 26, 27, 28, 40, 63, 64, 66, 67, 70, 71, 74, 75, 78, 79, 80, 81, 82, 83, 118, 120, and are the copyright of the author.

The remaining pictures are reproduced by permission of the following: Alinari-Giraudon, 90; British Museum, 37; Department of Astronomy, University of Michigan, 85; Escher Association, 38 and 39; Galerie Denise René, Paris, 76; Griffith Institute, 126; Hirmer Fotoarchiv, 89; D.H. Hubel and T.H. Wiesel and the *Journal of Physiology*, 12; Ronald C. James, 1; Lowell Observatory, 108; Museum of Fine Arts, Boston, gift of Edward W. Forbes, 91; Douglas Mazonowicz, 121; E.H. Gombrich and Phaidon Press, London, 17 and 18; George Rainbird, London, 88; Man Ray, 103 and 104; Rizzoli Editore, Milan, 46; Science Museum, London, 84, 86, 107, 109, 110, 111, 133 and 134; Tate Gallery, London, and Bridget Riley, 77; David Diringer and Thames and Hudson, London, 122, 123 and 124.

Directions for viewing the 3-D pictures and performing the experiments in this book

The 3-D (stereo) pictures

In order to see these in three dimensions, the reader should wear the red-green spectacles to be found at the back of the book. These colours are matched to the red and green inks of the stereo pictures so that one half of each stereo pair is visible only to the appropriate eye.

By reversing the glasses, the right eye sees the left eye's picture and vice-versa. Switching the eyes over in this way can reveal some interesting facts. It will be found that the figures change shape, illustrating how apparent distance can affect apparent size, by a scaling mechanism in the brain.

The reader may find it interesting to move his head around, or tilt the book, while viewing the stereo pictures. They will go through strange shape transformations and will appear to remain 'aimed' at the observer as he moves.

The glasses are also used to route different parts of figures to each eye: for illustrating retinal rivalry (figure 74), and the effect of sharing parts of illusion figures between the eyes (figure 75).

Making a depth-ambiguous object

A major theme of the book is the difference between seeing objects and seeing pictures of objects. Much of this is illustrated with skeleton cube objects and various kinds of pictures of cubes. Just because object and picture perception are so different, it is impossible to illustrate object-perception at all adequately. The reader is recommended to construct a skeleton cube for himself. This may be made of wire or by glueing together matches or, preferably, cocktail sticks as these are somewhat longer. Ideally the skeleton cube should be painted matt black, but this is not essential. Its appearance when visually reversed is so extraordinary that the slight effort of making one is fully justified by the result.

The spiral disk (on page 189) may be cut out and placed on a record-player turntable to rotate it at constant speed. To induce an after-effect of movement, the centre of the disk should be fixated for up to 30 seconds.

The Benham's disk (on page 191) should produce a number of subjective colours when rotated. I have designed this disk specially to work at the low speeds of a record-player turntable. It may be best to spin the turntable gently by hand – if this can be done without damaging it – to try the effect of a variety of speeds. The reader may experiment with various kinds of lighting to get the most saturated colours from black and white.

1 Objects and pictures

We are surrounded by objects. Our lives are spent identifying, classifying, using and judging objects. Objects are tools, shelter, weapons; they are food; they are things precious, beautiful, boring, frightening, lovable . . . almost everything we know. We are so used to objects, to seeing them wherever we look, that it is quite difficult to realise that they present any problem. But objects have their existence largely unknown to the senses. We sense them as fleeting visual shapes, occasional knocks against the hand, whiffs of smell – sometimes stabs of pain leaving a bruise-record of a too-close encounter. What we experience is only a small part of what matters about objects. What matters is their 'physical properties', which allow bridges to stay up, and car engines to run, though the insides are hidden. The extraordinary thing is how much we rely on properties of objects which we seldom or never test by sensory experience.

It has sometimes been thought that behaviour is controlled by information immediately available to the eyes and other senses. But sensory information is so incomplete – is it adequate to guide us among surrounding objects? Does it convey all that we need to know about an object in order to behave to it appropriately? At once we see the difficulty – the continuous problem the brain has to solve. Given the slenderest clues to the nature of surrounding objects we identify them and act not so much according to what is directly sensed, *but to what is believed.* We do not lay a book on a 'dark brown patch' – we lay it on a table. To belief, the table is far more than the dark brown patch sensed with the eyes; or the knock with the knuckle, on its edge. The brown patch goes when we turn away; but we accept that the table and the book remain.

Bishop Berkeley (1685–1753) questioned whether objects in fact continue to exist when not sensed – for what evidence could there be? But rather than allow objects to have, as Bertrand Russell puts it, 'a jerky life', he supposed that they exist continuously because God is always observing them, which Berkeley used as an argument for the existence of God. His doubt, and later certainty, are expressed in Ronald Knox's famous limerick and reply:

There was a young man who said, 'God
Must think it exceedingly odd
  If He finds that this tree
  continues to be
When there's no one about in the Quad.'

Dear Sir:
  Your astonishment's odd:
I am always about in the Quad.
  And that's why the tree
  Will continue to be,
Since observed by
  Yours faithfully G O D

Berkeley's doubt raises an important question: what can we *know* beyond sensation?

The optical images in the eyes are but patterns of light: unimportant until used to read non-optical aspects of things. One cannot eat an image, or be eaten by one – in themselves images are biologically trivial. The same is not, however, true for all sensory information. The senses of touch and taste do signal directly important information: that a neighbouring object is hard or hot, food or poison. These senses monitor characteristics immediately important for survival: important no matter what the object may be. Their information is useful before objects are identified. Whether the hand is burned by a match, a soldering-iron or boiling water makes little difference – it is rapidly withdrawn in any case. What matters is the burning heat, and this is directly monitored. The nature of the object may be established afterwards. Such responses are primitive – pre-perceptual reactions, not to objects but to physical conditions. Recognising objects, and behaving appropriately to their hidden aspects, comes later.

In the evolution of life the first senses must have been those which monitor physical conditions which are immediately important for survival. Touch, taste and temperature senses must have developed before eyes: for visual patterns are only important when interpreted in terms of the world of objects. But this requires an elaborate nervous system (indeed almost a metaphysics) if behaviour is controlled by belief in what the object is rather than directly by sensory input.

A curious hen-and-egg type of question arises: which came first, the eye or the brain? For what use is an eye without a brain capable of using visual information – but then why should a 'visual' brain develop before there were eyes to feed it with visual information?

What may have happened is that the primitive touch

nervous system was taken over to serve the first eyes, the skin being sensitive not to touch only but also to light. The visual sense probably developed from a response to moving shadows on the surface of the skin – which would have given warning of near-by danger – to recognition of patterns when eyes developed optical systems. The stages seem to have been, first a concentration of specially light-sensitive cells localised at certain regions, and then 'eye pits', the light-sensitive cells forming the bottom of gradually deepening pits which served to increase the contrast of shadows at the light-sensitive regions, by shielding them from ambient light. The lens most probably started as a transparent window, protecting the eye pits from being blocked by small particles floating in the sea in which the creatures lived. The protective windows may have gradually thickened in their centres, for this would at first increase the intensity of light on the sensitive cells until – dramatically – the central thickening produced an image-forming eye: to present optical patterns to the ancient touch nervous system.

Touch can be signalled in two quite distinct ways. When an object is in contact with an area of skin, its shape is signalled from many touch receptors, down many parallel nerve fibres simultaneously to the central nervous system. But shape can also be signalled with a single moving finger, or probe, exploring shapes by tracing them in time. A moving probe can not merely signal the two-dimensional shape that happens to be in contact, but can trace shapes in three dimensions, though it will take a considerable time to do so. Also, if the object it is exploring is itself alive, it will certainly give the game away – as we know by being tickled.

Touch is not a secret sense, and it is limited to objects in physical contact. This means that when a foe is identified by touch, it is too late to devise and carry out a strategy. Immediate action is demanded, and this cannot be subtle or planned. Eyes give warning of the future, by signalling distant objects. It seems very likely that brains as we know them could not have developed without senses – particularly eyes – capable of providing advance information, by signalling the presence of distant objects. As we shall see, eyes require intelligence to identify and locate objects in space, but intelligent brains could hardly have developed without eyes. It is not too much to say that eyes freed the nervous system from the tyranny of reflexes, leading to strategic planned behaviour and ultimately to abstract thinking. We are still dominated by visual concepts. Our problem now is to understand the world of objects without being limited by what we have learned through the senses.

1 *left*. Retinal images are patterns in the eye – patterns made up of light and dark shapes and areas of colour – but we do not see patterns, we see objects. We read from pictures in the eye the presence of external objects: how this is achieved is the problem of perception. Objects appear separate, distinct; and yet as pictures on the retina they may have no clear boundaries. In this photograph of a spotted dog, most half-tones have been lost (as in vision by moonlight) and yet we can distinguish the spots making up the dog from similar spots of the background. To make this possible there must be stored information in the brain, of dogs and thousands of other objects.

The data that most philosophers consider are limited to sensory experience. This is not so for physics, which accepts data from instruments capable of monitoring characteristics of the world quite unknown before instruments were invented. Radio and X-rays were totally unknown to brains until less than a century ago: they have changed our intellectual view of the world, though not sensed directly. This presents something of a paradox for empiricist philosophy, for science uses 'observational data' which can only be 'observed' with instruments: so the senses can no longer be said to be the sole source of direct knowledge.

Since perception is a matter of reading non-sensed characteristics of objects from available sensory data, it is difficult to hold that our perceptual beliefs – our basic knowledge of objects – is free of theoretical contamination. We not only believe what we see: to some extent we see what we believe.

A central problem of visual perception is how the brain interprets the patterns of the eye in terms of external objects. In this sense 'patterns' are very different from 'objects'. By a pattern we mean some set of inputs, in space or time, at the receptor. This is used to indicate and identify external objects giving rise to the sensory pattern. But what we perceive is far more than patterns – we perceive *objects* as existing in their space and time.

An initial problem is how objects are distinguished from their surroundings. This problem becomes clear if we look at a picture where the object is difficult to distinguish. Figure 1 is a photograph of a spotted dog against a dappled background – it is quite difficult to see the dog. Contours and differences of texture or colour help, but quite often boundaries of objects are not sharp and colour differences can be misleading. There is a similar problem in hearing speech or music. Words sound distinct from each other, but physically they are not separated. Physically they run into each other, just as the images of objects do upon the retina. Objects are somehow extracted from the continuous patterns at the receptors.

There is a well-known visual effect: 'figure-ground reversal'. Figure 2 shows a face – or does it? Here perception fluctuates between two possibilities. This is important, for it shows at once that perception is not simply determined by the patterns of excitation at the retina. There must be subtle processes of interpretation, even at this elementary level.

The psychologist whose name is associated with figure-ground reversal is the Dane, Edgar Rubin. He used simple but cunningly contrived line drawings in which a pair of shapes, either of which taken alone would be seen as an object of some kind, share a common border-line. What

2. This is seen sometimes as a face, sometimes as something else. Perception fluctuates between two clearly defined possibilities. This is an example of visual 'reversal', by the Danish psychologist, Edgar Rubin.

happens is that, when joined, each competes with the other. Alternatively, one is relegated to mere background, and hardly seen, while the other dominates as object: then this one fades perceptually away to become for a time mere background in its turn. This spontaneous alternation of figure and ground is a curious effect. It shows something of the dynamic nature of perceptual processes.

There are many subtle effects related to figure-ground reversal. When a region becomes figure, it generally looks quite different. Of figure 3 Rubin says:

One can experience alternately a radially marked or concentrically marked cross. If the concentric cross is seen as figure after the radial one, it is possible to note a characteristic change in the concentric markings which depends on whether they belong to the figure or the ground. When they are part of the ground, they do not appear interrupted. On the contrary, one has the impression that the concentric circles continue behind the figure. Nothing of this kind is noticed when the concentrically marked sectors compose that which is seen as figure.

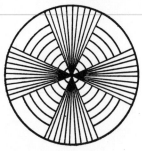

3. One of Rubin's figure/ground reversing figures. Here, there are two equally held figures, which in turn are relegated to 'ground'. Regions accepted as 'figure' are subtly changed perceptually, as described by Rubin in the quotation.

4. Rubin's most striking example of visual reversal. This is seen, alternatively, as a pair of faces 'looking at each other' and as a vase.

Rubin was well aware of the significance of his demonstration-experiments to the problem of how we see objects, though curiously this aspect of his work was largely ignored by later writers. Rubin says in this connection:

When a reversal of figure and ground occurs, one can observe that the area affected by the shape-giving function of the contour at the same time obtains a characteristic which is similar to that which leads one to call objects 'things'. . . . Even when the figure does not look like any known thing, it can still have this thing-character. By 'thing-character' we mean a similarity to what is common to all experienced objects . . .

So we have a hint as to how we might discover the kinds of features used by the brain to make this decision: what are objects, and what is space between the objects? This hint has still not been fully followed up.

Rubin's most striking example is given in figure 4. This is seen alternately as a pair of faces 'looking at each other' and as a vase, which becomes the space between the faces when they are object. Seeing the vase perceptually fade away, to be replaced by the pair of faces emerging from sinister shadows is a queer, almost frightening, experience. Rubin says of this figure:

The reader has the opportunity not only to convince himself that the ground is perceived as shapeless but also to see that a meaning read into a field when it is figure is not read in when the field is seen as ground.

5. The same reversal occurs whether the faces are black and the space between – the vase – is white, or whether the faces are white and the vase black.

He considers some implications to art, especially the emotional significance of pictures. Again the significance is given not by the stimulus pattern directly but by the interpretation put upon it. As he says charmingly:

If a figure looks like a beloved and admired professor from his homeland, this may remind the subject of the pleasure in having met him again as he stopped by on the way to Göttingen. If a figure looks like a beautiful female torso, this indubitably calls forth certain feelings.

17

Extending this to works of art:

When one succeeds in experiencing as figure areas which are intended as ground, one can sometimes see that they constitute aesthetically displeasing forms. If one has the misfortune in pictures of the Sistine Madonna to see the background as figure, one will see a remarkable lobster claw grasping Saint Barbara, and another odd pincer-like instrument seizing the holy sexton.

Unfortunately we still do not know in detail which are the features which *prevent* figure-ground (or 'object-space') reversal. These are, however, important. Small areas enclosed in larger areas are taken as figure, or object. Repeated pattern is taken as belonging either to figure or to ground but not to both. Straight lines are attributed to figure. Emotionally-toned shapes are also attributed to figure and, when present, tend to make figure dominant. In addition, the observer's perceptual 'set' and his individual interests can bias the situation.

Rubin used line drawings almost exclusively for his perceptual experiments, as did almost all psychologists until recently. But as we will try to show, pictures are in some ways highly artificial inputs for the eye. Although we can learn a lot about perception from pictures, and they are certainly convenient for providing stimulus patterns, they are a very special kind of object which can give quite atypical results. Object-space reversals can take place (for example when we look at roofs of houses against an evening sky) as well as the figure-ground reversals described by Rubin for pictures.

Object-space reversals merit further study, for what happens as we gradually introduce more data showing that a certain shape *is* an object?

How are some patterns established as representing objects? The problem is acute, for we often see patterns without attributing 'thingness' to them. We see patterns of leaves, of clouds, of fine or coarse texture on the ground. The decorative arts present formal or random patterns, which we may see as patterns not as objects. True, we may almost 'see' Queen Victoria in a cloud formation, or a wicked face, fleetingly, in the flickering flames of a fire. We may see as it were *hints* of objects in patterns, and random shapes, but we certainly can see patterns without accepting them as objects.

The Gestalt psychologists, in the early part of the century, made much play of 'perceptual organisation': that there are Principles, largely inherited, by which stimulus patterns are organised into 'wholes' (*Gestalten*). This organising into 'wholes' was demonstrated with

6. Simple dot patterns were used by the Gestalt psychologists to investigate their 'Principles of perceptual organization'. We may think of these as primary stages in perception – the linking of data from retinal patterns in terms of probable objects. This may be regarded as like a detective gathering and combining available clues used for making decisions on who is the criminal – or in perception, what is the *object*? This figure illustrates how points close together are seen to 'belong' to each other: the pattern is seen as *pairs* of dots.

black and white figures, mainly patterns composed of dots. The point is that even an array of random dots tends to form 'configurations'. It is almost impossible to see three dots, with any spacing, without also seeing at the same time a triangle. In a random array we see triangles, squares, rows – all sorts of figures emerge. Patterns of dots were used to try to establish Laws of Organisation. These were discussed in a classical paper by Max Wertheimer, entitled: 'Principles of Perceptual Organisation' (1923). Wertheimer presented several patterns, such as figure 6, and pointed out that they are seen as groups of dots, the closer dots forming perceptual pairs. They are seen as 'belonging' to each other.

Another example given was figure 7. Each sloping line forms a 'unit'. They may also combine to form sloping rectangles. This shows that *proximity* is a factor in perceptual grouping.

7. Another example of grouping of dots by *proximity*. This figure is generally seen as sloping triads of dots, also as oblique rectangles.

8. This is seen as a series of rows, the identical symbols being perceptually linked. This illustrates the importance of *similarity* in perceptual organisation.

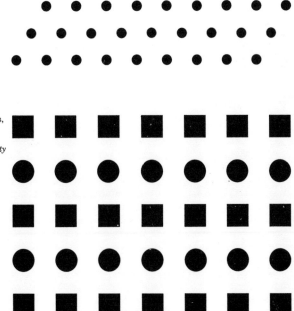

Another Principle is shown in figure 8. The circles and the squares are seen separately, each forming rows. This demonstrates that *similarity* is a factor in perceptual grouping. The Gestalt writers put a lot of weight on what they called 'good figure', and 'closure'; by this they meant properties such as geometrical simplicity, particularly approximations of circles, tending to 'organise the parts into wholes of these shapes'. Considering movement, 'common fate' was regarded as important – that related movement of parts makes the parts cohere into a 'whole'.

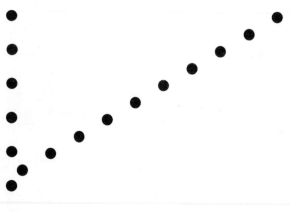

9. This shows that there is more to perceptual 'grouping' than proximity. The lowest dot of the oblique row is closest to the dots in the vertical row. Evidently the tendency to organise dots into rows is stronger than the tendency of association by proximity.

To the Gestalt writers, these Organising Principles were innate, inherited. They gave very little weight to individual past experience. Clear evidence of perceptual learning was perhaps lacking at that time and there were reasons, stemming from the contemporary German metaphysics, which made emphasis on innateness attractive. But it is perfectly possible to accept their observations as valid while denying that they are due to innate organising principles. There is no strong argument against saying that most objects are rather simple, and closed in shape, that the parts of objects move together, that objects often have repeated structure or texture patterns – and so on. In short, there seems no evidence against supposing that the organising principles represent attempts to make objects out of patterns – typical object characteristics being favoured – and the 'Principles' were developed by inductive generalisation from instances. Since we all experience essentially similar objects it would not be too surprising if we developed similar, even identical, generalisations. Although this was considered by some of the Gestalt writers it was rejected, though not for reasons that we would now accept as having any force. But possibly they were right, pos-

sibly there are innate tendencies to organising parts into wholes. This would still be accepted by some writers, though the general Gestalt philosophy is very largely rejected as being an extreme case of non-explanation.

It is probably fair to say that the Gestalt writers were more interested in how we see patterns than in how we see objects, for they generally used highly artificial visual material, such as the dot patterns.

Wertheimer claims that:

Perceptual organisation occurs from above to below; the way in which parts are seen, in which the sub-wholes emerge, in which grouping occurs, is not an arbitrary, piecemeal and-summation of elements, but is a process in which characteristics of the whole play a major determining role.

But if this were true in normal perception, we might expect that the world would look like a wobbly jelly.

Granted that organising into 'wholes' is important, it is easy to find examples of where this must be due to individual past experience. For example, we find it in grouping letters in a language – which is most certainly learned. There used to be an English comedian, who called himself

10. Lines of dots (or solid lines) which converge, are perceptually organised in three dimensions. Normal objects exist and are seen in three-dimensional space, though pictures – including retinal images – are flat. Converging features are generally taken to indicate depth by perspective shrinking of the image with increasing distance. For normal retinal images this is a good bet, but in pictures the convergence of perspective is presented to the eye on the flat plane of the picture – making pictures essentially paradoxical. Here the organisation is appropriate to normal three-dimensional space and not to the converging dots which lie on the flat plane of the page. They are organised in terms of normal space rather than the picture-plane.

11 *opposite*. This oblique camera angle of a textured surface gives a compelling impression of a slanting surface. The bricks are seen as slanting, yet the page on which the picture lies is not – and does not appear to be – slanting. This double reality is part of the paradox of pictures.

NOSMO KING. This was not in fact his real name. He 'discovered' it one day seeing, written across a double door at the theatre: NO SMOKING. When the doors opened he saw his new name appear.

This was anticipated by Helmholtz, the great German physicist (1821–94), when he argued for individual learning as important for perception, in the following:

There are numerous illustrations of fixed and inevitable associations of ideas due to frequent repetition, and even when they have no natural connections, but are dependent merely on some conventional arrangement, as, for example, the connection between written letters in a word and its sound and meaning. . . . Facts like these show the widespread influence that experience, training and habit have on our perceptions.

Few would disagree with him, but there remains the possibility that some perceptual organising processes are 'wired in' at birth. For reasons of economy, we might expect it. At any rate it is now clear from neurological studies that some visual feature-detectors are built in to retina and brain structure. This has been established over the last ten years from direct electrical recording from individual nerve cells of the eye and the brain.

When the electrical activity of local regions of a frog's retina are recorded from electrodes placed in excised eyes, it is found that only a few features of the pattern of stimulation on the retina are represented in terms of neural activity, and so signalled to the brain. Signals are given when the stimulus light is changed in intensity – some cells signalling when it is switched on, others when it is switched off, while others signal any change. (They are known as 'on', 'off' and 'on-off' receptors.) Receptors signalling changes of illumination are probably responsible for signalling movement, which is vital for the frog for detecting and catching flies; as indeed it is to all animals for survival, since movement is generally associated with potential food or danger. At the first stage of visual perception – the retina – we find neural mechanisms responding to specific patterns in space or time. In a delightful paper, 'What the Frog's Eye Tells the Frog's Brain', by Lettvin, Maturana, McCulloch and Pitts, several specific pattern-receptive mechanisms are identified. The eye responds to movement, to changes of illumination and to what we may call 'rotundity'. A small black shadow is signalled strongly and serves to evoke the fly-catching reflex. This 'bug-detector' gives an immediate response – the tongue shooting out for fly-catching – without loss of time by information processing

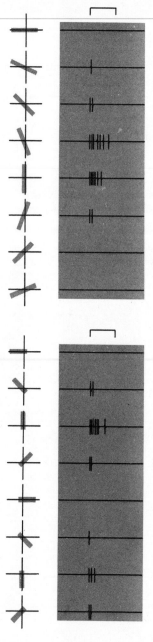

by the brain. The frog's brain receives but few kinds of pattern information from its eyes. In general as brains develop up the evolutionary scale eyes signal more information and become simpler. The retina is not merely a layer of light-sensitive cells, it is also a 'satellite computer' in which visual information is pre-processed for the brain. Vital information, such as movement, is extracted and signalled directly by the retina in eyes as highly developed as the rabbit and, most likely, in our own.

A really basic discovery was made by two American neurophysiologists, D. Hubel and T. N. Wiesel, some ten years ago. Placing micro-electrodes in the 'visual brain' (the *area striata* of the occipital cortex) of the cat, they found that certain brain cells respond to specific patterns at the eye, other brain cells to other patterns. Some cells responded to movement in one direction but not the opposite or any very different direction; other cells responded to lines oriented at a certain angle; others to corners. Activity at the surface of this region of cortex corresponds rather crudely to the spatial position of stimulation of the retina – a rough electrical spatial map is projected on the occipital cortex from the eye – but deeper down spatial position is lost and patterns are represented by the firing of a few cells regardless of position on the eye.

More recently Hubel and Wiesel have found that pattern information of various kinds is brought together in 'columns' arranged at right angles to the clearly visible layers of the striate cortex. These functional columns were discovered with subtle techniques as they are invisible to the eye. They seem to solve the problem of how the brain relates together not only three spatial dimensions but also colour, movement and other object-characteristics. A simple map would be quite inadequate, for there are insufficient spatial dimensions to represent more than the three spatial dimensions of external objects – since the brain is itself an object in normal three-dimensional space.

It seems from the electrophysiological data that perceptions are built from neural mechanisms responding to certain simple shapes, movement and colour. These are combined in the newly discovered cortical 'columns'. This is – logically – something like letters being combined to form words: the selected features are evidently basic units of the perceptual 'language' of the brain. What is not at all clear is how – to continue the language analogy – the neural 'words' are combined to form perceptual 'sentences'. It is not known at the neurological level how the outputs from the 'columns' are combined to give

12 *opposite*. This basic experiment by D.Hubel and T.N.Wiesel shows the activity of a single cell of the visual cortex of the brain as it is affected by a simple shape at the eye – a line at various orientations. The animal, a cat, views the (grey) line at various orientations. The selected cell whose activity is being recorded (shown by the spikes of electrical activity) fires at a certain orientation of the line at the eyes. Other cells respond to other orientations; others to movement; others to changing illumination. The features to which various cells respond form the 'words' of the brain's perceptual 'language', which is organised by what may be called the 'grammar of perception'. Electrophysiological experiments are beginning to tie up with psychological experiments. We begin to see how the pictures in the eyes are represented, or described, by brain activity.

Recently, Hubel and Wiesel have shown that many sensed characteristics are brought together in functional 'columns' in the brain, arranged at right angles to the layers of the *striate* area.

object-perception. We may guess that there is an intimate connection with memory stores, but at the present time how memory is stored is not known. It is not even known whether single cells store units of memory, or whether memories are stored as patterns involving very many cells, possibly by a process similar to the storing of optical patterns by holography and unlike the usual point-to-point representation as in normal photography. The answers to these questions remain for the future, but meanwhile it is worth preparing the ground by considering the phenomena of perception. Neurophysiological explanation is not everything. The activity of the nervous system cannot be interpreted without knowing what functions are served. Many useful explanations are in terms of function rather than in terms of underlying structure and activity within this structure. For example, the computer engineer does not have to know much physics to understand computer circuits; and the mathematician does not have to understand much electronics to understand their logic and use them. (To say, 'I understand why she went off with Bill', may be perfectly meaningful without any knowledge of what – in physical terms – went on in her brain.)

At this point we might be tempted into thinking that perception is simply a matter of combining activity from various pattern-detecting systems, to build up neural 'descriptions' of surrounding objects. But perception cannot be anything like as simple, if only because of a basic problem confronting the perceptual brain – the ambiguity of sensory data. The same data can always 'mean' any of several alternative objects. But we experience but one, and generally correctly. Clearly there is more to it than the putting together of neurally represented patterns to build perceptions, for decisions are required. We should look at the ambiguity of objects to see this more clearly. Establishing that a given region of pattern represents an object and not background is only a first step in the perceptual process. We are left with the vital decision: *What (kind of) object is this?*

The problem is acute because any two-dimensional image could represent an *infinity of possible three-dimensional shapes*. Often there are extra sources of information available; for example stereoscopic vision, or changing parallax as the head moves, but the fact remains that we can nearly always arrive at a reasonably reliable solution to the problem: 'What object is this?' Even though the number of possibilities is infinite.

Some shapes are seen, at different times, in more ways than one. Just as the object-space reversible figures spontaneously change, so some shapes though continuously identified as object yet spontaneously change as to *what* object it is, or what position it is being viewed from. Here we must discuss the work of the psychologist who has devised the most striking demonstrations based on the essential ambiguity of objects – Adelbert Ames.

Ames started out as a painter, but ended by devising many of the best known 'visual demonstrations'. It has not, however, always been made clear what they demonstrate. Unfortunately Ames himself wrote very little: he was a visual man.

Ames made several models (sometimes full scale) designed to give the same retinal image as familiar objects, though the models were in fact of very different shapes. The models gave the same image as the familiar object only from one critical view point, and for a single eye. The best-known demonstration is the 'Ames room'. This gives the same image to an eye placed at the critical position as a normal rectangular room – but in fact it is very far from rectangular. The further wall recedes to one side, so that one of the far corners is much further from the eye than the other corner; but both corners subtend the same angle at the eye placed in the critical position; for as the further wall recedes it gets correspondingly larger. The Ames room is simply one of an

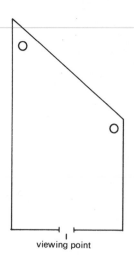

viewing point

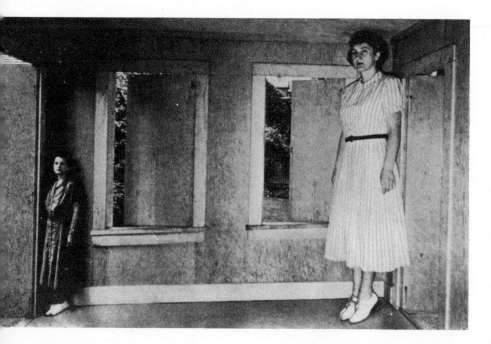

infinite set of three-dimensional shapes giving the same image to the (critically placed) eye that it would receive from a normal rectangular room.

As a matter of fact, Ames was not the first to consider such a situation. Helmholtz suggested such a room fifty years before when he wrote:

Looking at the (normal) room with one eye shut, we think we see it just as distinctly and definitely as with both eyes. And yet we should get exactly the same view in case every point in the room were shifted arbitrarily to a different distance from the eye, provided they all remained on the same lines of sight.

Ames was, however, probably the first actually to *make* such a 'distorted' room, and he was the first to consider what would happen if one placed objects of familiar size inside – actually at different but apparently the same distance from the eye. What happens is shown in figure 14. This is a view from the critical position of an Ames room, with two people inside. One looks smaller than the other though in fact they are the same actual height. The apparently smaller person is about twice as far from the camera as the other, and so the image at the camera (or at an eye in this position) is half the size. So this is *not* a case of a visual distortion illusion (cf. page 74). It is that we trade size and distance wrongly in this situation.

Clearly the room without the people or other objects in it *must* look like a normal rectangular room – for it gives the same image at the eye. Perhaps, indeed, Helmholtz decided that to make a 'distorted' room would merely demonstrate the obvious. But adding the objects inside changes the situation; for now the eye is presented with a betting problem: 'Is the *room* an odd shape, or are the *people* odd sizes?' It is an experimental result, not to be anticipated, that observers continue seeing the room as normal (which it is not) and the people as different heights (which they are not). The odds have been rigged, and the brain makes the wrong bet. It loses; so we are fooled. The odds are easily changed: it has been reported that a newly married wife will not see her husband shrink as he walks across the room, but instead will see the room more or less its true peculiar shape. No doubt this effect might be used for calibrating wives.

If the room is explored with a long stick, it will gradually come to look its true queer shape. Such active exploration with a stick will correct the visual perception – though intellectual knowledge of the true shape of the room will not. It is an effort to get perceptual and intellectual knowledge to coincide. If the eighteenth-century empiricists had known this, philosophy might

13 *opposite above*. The Ames room – how it is made. It is a highly non-rectangular shape, but so designed that it gives the same retinal image (or photograph) from a critical view point as a normal rectangular room. (A picture, indeed, is an extreme case of the same thing, the picture being flat though it may give the same image to the eye as normal three-dimensional objects.) The Ames room is not flat, but is a queer-shaped room such that with increasing distance there is a corresponding increase in size, to give the image of a normal rectangular room. If made correctly, it *must* look like a normal room, for it gives the same image to the eye. What is interesting is what happens when we put objects, especially people, inside it. Do they – or the room – look odd?

14 *opposite below*. The Ames room – how it appears. The right-hand person looks much taller than the other. They are in fact the same height, but present different sizes to the eye. The further wall recedes, towards the left (as shown in figure 13). The left-hand person is twice as far from the camera as the other. Perspective is 'used backwards' to give the same retinal image as a normal rectangular room. So, apart from the figures, it *must* look the same as a rectangular room. (The question is, however: why does *any* room or other object look any *particular* shape?) This is an acute problem, because any projected image could be given by an infinity of differently shaped objects. The room is assumed (wrongly) to be rectangular, in which case the people must be very different in size. This shows how we base perception on bets. This is not a 'distortion illusion'.

have taken a very different course. No doubt there are also implications for political theory and judgement.

Is this all there is to the matter? Not quite. The Ames room is an interesting and dramatic demonstration – but is it an experiment from which conclusions can be drawn? If so, it is odd, for where is the control situation? Has the perceptual effect of the queer-shaped room really been demonstrated with no control?

15 *above*. The Ames-room-without-the-room! The people are photographed just as in the Ames room but without the room. One is twice as distant as the other. Is this how they appear? Most observers report that the girl photographed as smaller (actually most distant) appears shrunk, though also somewhat more distant. If people look shrunk when their image is smaller without the Ames room, we should re-evaluate the significance of the Ames room experiment.

16 *above*. How the Ames-room-without-the-room picture was taken. The girls are actually at different distances from the camera, with a white background and a floor-level camera-view to reduce texture and perspective information of their distances. Before we know what happens

when information is removed, we cannot assess the effects of mis-leading or other information on perception. It is vital to know what assumptions we make and how these are modified by retinal information in various circum-stances.

The question to ask, surely, is: what happens in the Ames room *without the room*? In other words – if we take two people with a blank background, and place one at twice the distance of the other with no visual information of their relative distances – does the more distant one look the same distance but half the size? If not, what effect can we attribute to the Ames room?

Figure 15 shows two people, one placed at twice the distance of the other, so that their images differ in size just as in the Ames room picture. Also, a low camera angle has been used to prevent perspective information of their relative distances. This photograph is not a composite, and has not been touched up in any way. Most people looking at it say that the actually nearer person looks a little nearer, but also a lot larger. In other words, the size difference is *not* attributed purely to distance when the Ames room has been removed. So perhaps rather too much weight has been placed on what we may call the Ames addition to the Helmholtz situation.

Another demonstration is the Ames chair. This consists of several rods supported on thin wires, all converging to one point. The rods are viewed from this point of con-

17 and 18. The Ames chair: a collection of rods suspended in converging wires. From the point of convergence they give the same image as a chair – and so are seen as a chair – though from other positions they appear as a collection of disjointed rods.

vergence, the wires following perspective lines from the eye to the rods. The rods are so arranged that, from this point of view, they form the image of a chair. They are then seen as a (model) chair. From any other point of view, of course, they are seen as a collection of disjointed rods. This is interesting, but like the room with nothing in it, it *has* to work. If the model is made well enough, it *must* look the same as objects of different shape but giving the same image at the eye.

What is really remarkable is not so much that the Ames demonstrations work (in the absence of conflicting evidence, and the conflicting cases *are* very interesting), but that the perceptual system ever does settle for one interpretation of retinal images from normal objects. Perhaps this is what the demonstrations bring out. It is surely remarkable that out of the infinity of possibilities the perceptual brain generally hits on just about the best one.

We are forced, at this early stage, to suppose that perception involves betting on the most probable interpretation of sensory data, in terms of the world of objects.

Perception involves a kind of inference from sensory data to object-reality. Further, behaviour is not controlled directly by the data, but by the solutions to the perceptual inferences from the data. This is clear from common experience: if I put a book on a table I do not prod the table first to check that it is solid. I act according to the *inferred* physical object – table – not according to the brown patch in my eye. So perception involves a kind of problem-solving – a kind of intelligence.

Helmholtz spoke of perception in terms of 'unconscious inferences'. For reasons not altogether clear to the present writer, this has never been very popular among psychologists. Helmholtz was particularly concerned with the fact that though sensory activity starts at surfaces of the body, including the retina, we experience 'things out there'. Also, illusions of 'out-thereness' can be extraordinarily powerful. For example, a dark room lit by a bright electronic flash will give an intense after-image in which every detail of the room is visible. Now although we know it is but a 'photograph' from the flash, on the eye, and though we turn round or walk out of the door with our after-image – yet we cannot see it as anything but a real room while the after-image remains. Helmholtz supposed, though he did not put it quite like this, that the brain continually carries out 'unconscious inference' of the form:

(Nearly) all retinal activity received is due to external objects.
This is retinal activity.
Therefore this is (probably) due to an external object.

At this point we must be clear that there is no 'little man inside' doing the arguing, for this leads to intolerable philosophical difficulties. Helmholtz certainly did not think this, but his phrase 'unconscious inferences', and his description of perceptions as 'unconscious conclusions' did perhaps suggest, at the time, to people unfamiliar with computers, some such unacceptable idea. But our familiarity with computers should remove temptation towards confusion of this kind. For we no longer think of inference as a uniquely *human* activity involving consciousness.

Helmholtz described his 'unconscious inferences' in perception in the following words, which I quote at length:

The psychic activities that lead us to infer that there in front of us at a certain place there is a certain object of a certain character, are generally not conscious activities, but unconscious ones. In their result they are equivalent to a conclusion, to the extent that the observed action on our senses enables us to form an idea as to the possible cause of this action; although as a matter of fact, it is invariably simply the nervous stimulations that are perceived, that is, the actions, but never the external objects themselves. But what seems to differentiate them from a conclusion, in the ordinary sense of the word, is that a conclusion is an act of conscious thought. An astronomer, for example, comes to real conclusions of this sort, when he computes the positions of the stars in space, their distances etc., from the perspective images he has had of them at various times and as they are seen from different parts of the orbit of the earth. His conclusions are based on conscious knowledge of the laws of optics. In the ordinary acts of vision this knowledge of optics is lacking. Still it may be permissible to speak of the psychic acts of ordinary perception as unconscious conclusions, *thereby making a distinction of some sort between them and the so-called conscious conclusions. And while it is true that there has been, and probably always will be, a measure of doubt as to the similarity of the psychic activity in the two cases, there can be no doubt as to the similarity between the results of such unconscious conclusions and those of conscious conclusions.*

This book may almost be regarded as an extension of this passage from Helmholtz. It is clearly first of all vital for an animal to distinguish, from the patterns in its eyes, between what are objects in the field of view and what is the space between objects. It is then necessary for it to identify the objects, from their characteristic patterns. But, as we have said, objects are far more than patterns at the senses. And it is these other, non-sensed, characteristics which are important to the owners of eyes. Are objects inferred from patterns? In this book I propose to consider the inner 'logic' of perception. The main argument is that perception is a kind of problem-solving. Pictures are regarded as a remarkable invention, requiring special perceptual skills for seeing them, leading to abstract symbols and ultimately to written language. By considering the perception of objects represented in pictures and symbols (including the pictograms of early languages) I hope to show that our most abstract thinking may be a direct development of the first attempts to interpret the patterns in primitive eyes in terms of external objects.

2

The peculiarity of pictures

Pictures have a double reality. Drawings, paintings and photographs are objects in their own right – patterns on a flat sheet – and at the same time entirely different objects to the eye. We see both a pattern of marks on paper, with shading, brush-strokes or photographic 'grain', and at the same time we see that these compose a face, a house or a ship on a stormy sea. Pictures are unique among objects; for they are seen both as themselves and as some other thing, entirely different from the paper or canvas of the picture. Pictures are paradoxes.

No *object* can be in two places at the same time; no object can lie in both two- and three-dimensional space. Yet pictures are both visibly flat and three-dimensional. They are a certain size, yet also the size of a face or a house or a ship. Pictures are impossible.

No eyes before man's were confronted by pictures. Previously, all objects *in themselves* were important or could be safely ignored. But pictures, though trivial in themselves, mere patterns of marks, are important in showing *absent* things. Biologically this is most odd. For millions of years animals had been able to respond only to present situations and the immediate future. Pictures, and other symbols, allow responses to be directed to situations quite different from the present; and may give perceptions perhaps not even possible for the world of objects. Apart from pictures and other symbols, the senses direct and control behaviour according to the physical properties of surrounding objects – not to some other, real or imaginary, state of affairs. Perhaps man's ability to respond to absent imaginary situations in pictures represents an essential step towards the development of abstract thought. Pictures are perhaps the first step away from immediate reality; and without this, reality cannot be deeply understood.

The retinal images do not have the double reality of external pictures. We do not see them both as patterns and as representing something else. We read aspects of reality from the patterns in the eyes, but we do not *also* see our eyes' images. The images are pictures to another observer – someone looking into our eye with a suitable optical instrument – but to ourselves they are but one link in the information chain through the nervous system. We do not see our own retinal images any more than we see the neural activity in the optic nerve or visual regions of the brain. So retinal images, though they are pictures to an external observer, do not have the double reality of pictures to the owner of the eye.

The ability to read non-optical reality from the optical images in the eyes is the miracle of visual perception. What we see goes far beyond the evidence available to the eyes. When reading a kind of reality from pictures, we are performing a most remarkable kind of problem-solving, which is only partly similar to reading reality of normal objects from our retinal images. Pictures are by no means normal objects; but they are extraordinarily interesting to consider as very special objects of perception.

Pictures are flat projections of three-dimensional objects. But it is strictly impossible to compress three dimensions into two without loss of information. So pictures are always ambiguous in depth. The remarkable thing is that we are able to make any sense of them, for any projection is *infinitely* ambiguous: it could represent an infinity of different objects, but generally we see but one.

To understand the peculiarities of pictures we should be able, experimentally, to compare what we see when we look at normal objects with what we see when looking at pictures. To do this we must be able to look at an object directly, and at pictures of the same object. It would be possible to draw pictures of the test objects, and to draw them with various perspectives or other changes of view, but this would be tedious. We have a much neater solution. We will project our chosen objects as shadows. This is particularly convenient, for we can project objects from any angle of view, and with any perspective, or none (figure 19). Using a small bright light to cast the shadow of an object on to a screen, we see its plane projections exactly as for an eye placed at the point-source of light.

This trick of using shadows for producing projections of objects is extremely useful. We will make use of it for several experiments, which the reader could easily try for himself. For most purposes objects made of wire are best; they look like line diagrams and have the advantage that no parts are hidden, except in exceptional orientations.

When a circular wire model is placed parallel to the screen, it will give a circular shadow. But at other angles of tilt it will give an elliptical shadow. The more tilted the circular object, the more eccentric will be the elliptical projection. Now if we already know that the wire object is a circle, then we will see that the elliptical projection is representing a circle as seen from the side, although the

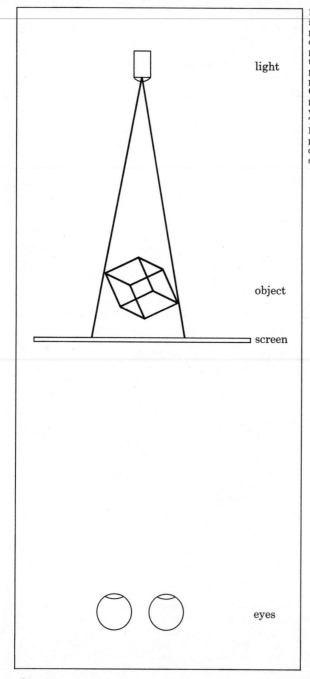

light

object

screen

eyes

19. Pictures – and retinal images – are essentially plane projections of objects in the field of view. For experimental purposes, it is highly convenient to cast shadows of objects from a point-source of light to give plane projections – pictures. Geometrically, this gives the projection an eye would receive when placed at the point-source. This can be better than using lenses, because the shadow projections have an infinite depth of field and the geometry is simple and exact.

retinal image is elliptical. But suppose we do not already know that it is a circle: then there is an infinite number of possibilities of eccentricity and tilt to give the *same* projection – the same image at the eye. The projection – and the retinal image – are infinitely ambiguous. So we cannot *strictly* know the object from its image, even when our life depends on it.

The same is true for more complex objects. Consider a skeleton cube (figure 20): the perspective projection shows one face – the nearer – as larger than the further face. The size difference may be great (when the shadow-casting

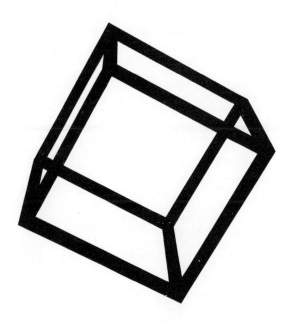

20. A wire skeleton cube placed in the light casts an accurate geometrical perspective shadow projection. By placing the object at various distances and orientations, we may see its corresponding plane projection, which is the same as the retinal image of an eye placed at the shadow-casting light. Although the faces are unequal in size, we generally see this as a cube. It is important to realise that the object giving this projection may in fact *not* be a cube. It could be a truncated pyramid, or indeed an infinity of other shapes; but we generally accept that it is some simple or familiar object.

light is close to the object) and yet the projection is generally judged to be that of a cube, with equal-sized faces and all angles right angles, though this is not so at the eye. We interpret the flat projection as a likely three-dimensional object even though it is very different from its picture.

There are deep implications here. Why do we see this projection as a cube – rather than one or more of the infinity of other shapes which could give this projection? It could, for example, be a projection of a topless ('truncated') pyramid – its smaller face nearer the shadow-casting light, or the eye. This different object could give precisely the same projection as the cube and yet we generally see it as a cube.

Evidently we have certain preferred 'answers' to the continual problem: What is the object giving this projection? We tend to choose the most likely objects. Cubes are commoner than topless pyramids, and we tend to see this projection as a cube though geometrically it could equally well be the topless pyramid, or an infinity of other shapes viewed from certain positions.

This acceptance by the brain of the most probable answer implies a danger: it must be difficult, perhaps sometimes impossible, to see very unusual objects; especially when they happen to give the same projection – the same picture – as probable, familiar, objects. But unusual shapes do occur and it might be important to see them correctly.

We are led at once to a fundamental way of thinking about perception. Perception is a matter of selecting the most likely object. But what are the possible objects selected from? Not from the actual world of objects. Retinal images evidently serve to select from a stored repertoire of objects represented symbolically in the 'visual' brain. Perception must, it seems, be a matter of seeing the present with stored objects from the past.

If visual characteristics are used to select from the brain's store of previously experienced objects – making sense of the world as best it can with its limited collection of answers from its past – then what happens when we are confronted with something unique? What happens when conflicting features are presented to the eye – as in a more-than-usually peculiar picture? Again what happens when the visual features which are used for selection of stored objects are inadequate for specifying one particular object? What happens if we present conflicting information: does a silly visual question give a silly perceptual answer?

By looking at pictures with such questions in mind (and admittedly this has little or nothing to do with pictures as an art form) we may use them for investigating the logic of perceptual problem-solving. But we must always remember that pictures are highly artificial – but then so are most laboratory experiments.

3

Ambiguous, paradoxical and uncertain figures

Ambiguous figures

Since there is always an infinite number of *possible* three-dimensional shapes which will give the same projection on a flat plane – the same picture – it is not surprising that perception can be uncertain, and ambiguous. The remarkable thing is that we are so seldom disturbed or misled by the ambiguity of the optical projection of objects upon the eye. When looking at normal objects we generally have the use of the two eyes to give the slightly different projections which, together, can resolve many depth ambiguities. Also, we have movement of the head which can in a similar way resolve ambiguities; but this is not available for pictures and yet we generally settle for one interpretation. There are exceptions. The exceptions show how the brain responds when it fails to settle for a single solution.

21. The Necker cube. This is the plane projection of a cube as seen from a great distance. There is no perspective size change. The figure is seen in spontaneously reversing depth. Evidently, there are two equally probable solutions to the perceptual problem: 'What is the object out there?' The brain entertains each of its hypothetical solutions in turn – and never makes up its mind.

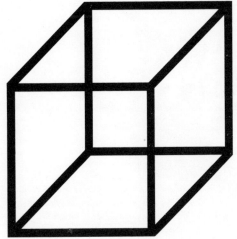

The best-known example is a skeleton cube, drawn without perspective so that no face is indicated by a size difference as nearer or further than another. This is the celebrated Necker cube, described by a Swiss crystallographer, L.A.Necker, in 1832. It has been discussed – in various terms – by psychologists ever since. It is a case where the retinal image could equally well be a projection of a familiar object viewed from either of two very different positions. In this case there are two likely solutions to the continuous perceptual problem: what – and where – is this object? Here there is no available information for making a choice. Rather than settling for one arbitrary solution the alternative likely hypotheses are entertained in turn: and the brain never makes up its mind (figure 21). Another example is Mach's figure, the skeleton half-open book (figure 22).

Ambiguity in depth is only one kind of ambiguity. It can also be uncertain what *kind* of object is represented by a picture, or by the retinal image of a normal object. It may even be uncertain whether *any* object is represented. We may be uncertain when looking at an 'abstract' painting: is the artist, however vaguely, representing *objects*? Perhaps not. Why should he represent them, if he doesn't wish to? Ink blots may suggest various objects – the basis of the Rorschach ink blot personality test – and it is not uncommon for cloud formations to 'look like' a face or a ship – or some other thing, though perhaps only by mystics are they confused (figure 23).

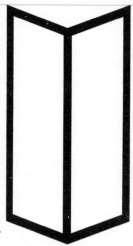

22. Mach's figure. Another example of a depth-reversing figure. It could be a book, the spine forward or backward.

23. Ink spot or object? The Rorschach personality test depends on the fact that we tend to 'see' objects even in the most ill-structured figures. The Necker cube has but two likely interpretations in terms of objects. An ink spot has an unlimited number, with no one highly probable. We tend to select objects which have interest: perceptual and personality differences may appear in the selection.

Figures can be designed (or can occur by chance) which are seen as two or more quite specific but different objects. The best-known example was designed by the American psychologist, E.G. Boring (figure 24). It looks sometimes like a charming young girl, sometimes like a frightening old woman; looking completely different in the alternative perceptions. As a young lady she is in profile, the lashes of one eye showing at her cheek. She wears a black band round her neck. As an old lady, the chin becomes a hideous

24. E.G. Boring's object-ambiguous mother-in-law. She is seen sometimes as a young girl, at other times as an old woman. These are the two most probable object interpretations of this figure, which are entertained in turn.

huge nose; the black band round the charming neck becomes the cruel mouth of a hag. It is quite fascinating to see the alternative perceptions in oneself of the same picture. Each feature changes significance so dramatically that it is hard to believe the picture has not objectively changed, by some trick.

This picture tends to remain stable until the eyes move to a different region. Certain regions tend to favour one perception, others the alternative. When the provocatively turned cheek becomes the beak-nose, the rest of the face seems to melt and change, following the lead of the nose: almost as the fair face of the good Dr Jekyll loses its identity to become the evil Mr Hyde.

Although changing the position of the eyes does tend to initiate a change of perception, and in some pictures such as the young-old woman one perception is favoured by looking at certain regions, it is not *necessary* to shift the gaze for a perceptual change to occur. It can be entirely spontaneous.

If either this picture or a Necker cube is looked at with a steady eye, it will still change though less often. The change can have a purely central origin in the brain and not be due to change of information at the eye. This is an extremely important point, as we shall see, and is further evidence of perception being an active process (or rather a complex set of processes) making sense of retinal images

25. A depth-ambiguous object (a skeleton cube) is held in the hand, to give visual and simultaneous touch information. In the experiment, the cube is coated with luminous paint to glow in the dark. It will reverse visually in spite of the touch information – then the visual and touch worlds separate. The effects are weird and well worth trying.

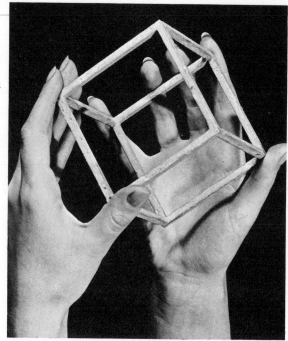

26 *opposite*. Adding a second point-source light, horizontally separated by 2½ in. from the first, we obtain a pair of plane projections each from a different view point, corresponding precisely to the view points of a pair of eyes placed at the point-sources. When an observer views the screen, with red and green glasses and corresponding red and green filters over the point-sources, one of his eyes will see the projection from one view point, the other eye from the other. These views are fused by his brain to give three-dimensional stereoscopic depth. He sees a three-dimensional structured shadow. (Polarising filters can be used instead of the coloured filters; often better for experimental purposes.) This technique allows us to bring back the second eye when viewing pictures, to establish the importance of stereo vision – especially for unfamiliar objects, when it is most important.

in terms of possible objects. It is not possible to hold the eyes quite steady: they jump from point to nearby point, and there is a high-frequency tremor at all times. But we know that these ambiguous figures still change perceptually even when the image is fixed *precisely* to the retina, so that though the eye may move the image does not shift. This can be done by optical means, but more simply with after-images. The reader can perform the experiment for himself, with no apparatus beyond a photographic flash.

Place the (normally ambiguous) figure at a convenient distance from the eyes, in a very dim room. Arrange an electronic flash to illuminate it. Looking carefully at the centre (or some chosen part) of the figure, fire the flash. After a few seconds, the figure will be seen as a vivid after-image. It may be 'projected' on to a sheet of white paper, or a wall, dimly lit.

It will be found that the figure as seen in the after-image still changes spontaneously. But the after-image is fixed precisely upon the retina: though the eye moves there is no shift between the effective image and retina.

The conclusion is that although eye movements (or blinking or sudden changes of illumination) can induce

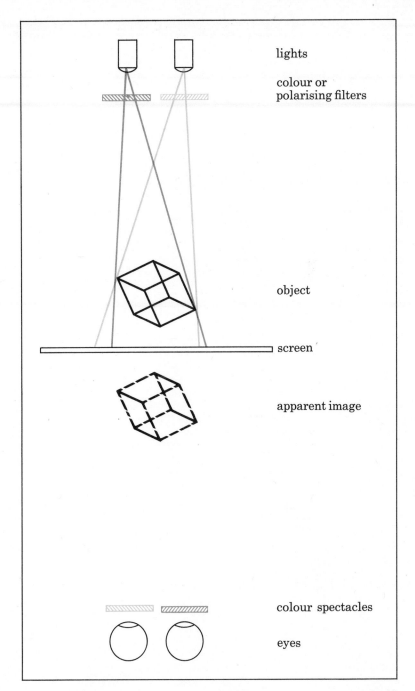

lights

colour or
polarising filters

object

screen

apparent image

colour spectacles

eyes

perceptual alternations, changes at the eye are not necessary: they *can*, and often do, occur spontaneously, representing spontaneous decision-processes of the brain.

What happens to these spontaneous changes when there
is *other* sensory information available for signalling the
true state of affairs to the brain? Little is known about
this, though some experiments have been performed by
the author with a colleague. In these experiments a three-
dimensional object was used – not a picture – so that
shape could be signalled by touch at the same time that it
was being *seen*.

The object used was a wire cube, painted with luminous
paint to glow in the total darkness of the experimental
room. The cube (which had 4 in. sides) was fixed rigidly to
a table by one corner and was actively felt throughout the
experiment, which consisted in simply reporting to a tape-
recorder which face appeared the nearer. This was done
for each observer, both with and without simultaneous
touch. It was found that all observers experienced reversals in depth in each condition of the experiment. Reversals occurred about half as often as normal with the added
touch information. When the cube reverses, the visual
and touch spaces separate: the faces of the cube *appear* in
one place but are *felt* in another. This is a curious
experience (figure 25).

Evidently visual interpretations of objects, at any rate
in the adult human observer, are selected largely on visual
information. Other sensory information such as touch
does influence how we see, but it does not determine
vision. Vision seems to be to a great extent autonomous in
the adult; even though, as we strongly suspect, it has its
origin both in evolution and in the developing child in
direct experience of objects from touch. But we need more
research to know just how much visual perception can be
affected and corrected by the other senses.

We have mentioned two kinds of ambiguity: the first
kind was the depth-ambiguity of figures, such as skeleton
cubes; the second kind was object-ambiguity of figures,
such as the young-old woman picture. It is useful to name
these as 'depth-ambiguity' and 'object-ambiguity' for they
are essentially different. We shall now devise experiments
for investigating them further, but we need rather different kinds of experiments. We shall start to investigate
depth-ambiguity, using simple experimental apparatus
which the interested reader could quite easily build for
himself. It reveals a surprising wealth of effects, which
may help us to understand visual perception of objects.
Essential to the approach is the discovery that we can get
these dramatic changes in perception though the information at the eye remains constant. This makes it possible, by

holding the eye's information constant, to investigate central perceptual decision-processes of the brain. Most important, we can discover something of how perceptual hypotheses – perceptions – are selected according to sensory data. This we regard as the central problem.

The Necker cube has no perspective. There are two faces of exactly equal size and shape which nevertheless are seen as front or back. A perspective drawing of a cube shows the nearer face as larger than the back face. This size difference is a cue to distance and so, we may suppose, it will tend to prevent the cube from reversing – if perspective reduces depth-ambiguity. By observing it and noting the total time over several minutes that it appears to lie in each orientation, we can establish the effect of perspective – or any other depth cue – on reducing and finally abolishing ambiguity.

It turns out that the reversal in depth is only one of several very curious effects. Other effects, which we will discover with these experiments, seem to distinguish between how the brain handles *pictures* and how it handles *objects*.

In addition to finding the effect of perspective, we shall also try to find the effect of adding the second eye – to give stereoscopic depth. Lastly, we shall consider what happens when movement is introduced.

We will compare perception of various kinds of picture with direct perception of the pictured object itself.

For these experiments, we must have a suitable technique for presenting objects as pictures of the various kinds we are considering. We must be able to present objects as pictures with any amount of perspective, including no perspective, and as three-dimensional pictures in stereo depth. It turns out that all this is quite simple by using shadows.

To do this we may develop the shadow-projection scheme already mentioned. The shadow projector can be made to give not only any perspective – including none – but can also add the view of the second eye to give stereoscopic depth. The apparatus is quite simple. It consists of a small light-source which casts a shadow of the object (such as a wire cube) on to a translucent screen. Optically, the eye is at the point-source: it gives a shadow projection the same as the image of an eye at that position, but presented flat upon the screen – so it is a picture. We have converted the object into a perspective picture. The amount of perspective is given simply by the distance of the light-source from the object. The closer the light, the greater the perspective. If the light were infinitely distant, there would be no perspective. However, rather than use very great distances for this, we use a large parabolic mirror to make all

27. The technique may be used to project models in enlarged 3-D to an audience, by projecting the pair of shadows on to a large screen. (The screen must be silver if cross-polarisation is used.)

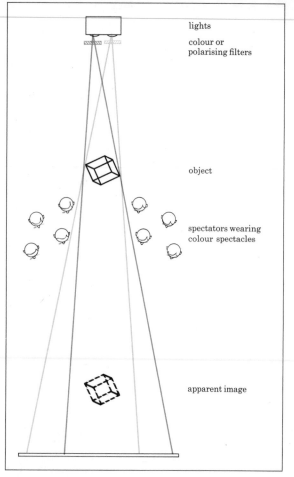

lights

colour or polarising filters

object

spectators wearing colour spectacles

apparent image

light parallel between the mirror and the screen. The light is placed at the distance of the mirror's focus.

The object can be placed in any position – or continuously rotated – to give an ever-changing view.

To add the second eye – to give stereoscopic pictures of our objects – we add a second point-source light. This is placed beside the first and separated by the distance of the eyes, about $2\frac{1}{2}$ in. This gives the two projections that the retinas of a pair of eyes would receive. The differences of view given by the horizontal separation of the lights is the same as the difference between the images of two eyes in that position, and so we have produced correct stereo-pair projections of the object (figure 27). We now only have

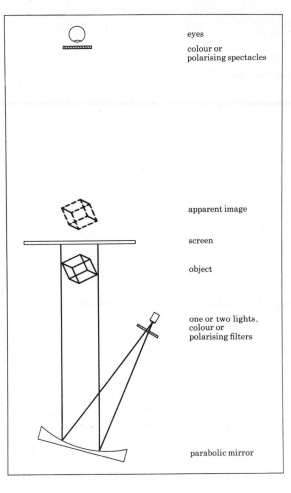

28. The pair of point-sources (only one shown) for stereo projection may be combined with the parabolic mirror which removes perspective. This gives three-dimensional projections but without perspective. Although impossible in real life, this is extremely useful for our experiments.

eyes

colour or
polarising spectacles

apparent image

screen

object

one or two lights,
colour or
polarising filters

parabolic mirror

to arrange things so that the right eye receives its correct projection and the left its projection. We must route one to each eye. This is done with crossed polarising or colour filters.

We will now compare what happens when we view an object *directly* with what happens when we view it as a *picture* – in each of our four projections. The perspective can be varied continuously, but we will use only (a) one perspective from a near view point, and (b) zero-perspective – an infinitely distant view point. We will use, at least for the moment, only two objects for these comparisons: the wire cube and the topless pyramid.

Figure 29	Figure 30
Spectator using one eye	**Spectator using one eye**

Mono-perspective	**Mono-perspective**
Object perception	**Picture perception**

The cube looks like a cube. Although the back face gives a smaller image at the eye, it does not *look* smaller. All the angles appear as right angles (though in the projection at the eye they are not so – for the projection at the eye is a *perspective projection*).

When the cube reverses (like the Necker cube) in depth, then *it no longer looks like a cube*. The apparent back looks too large and the front too small. It looks like a topless (truncated) pyramid. This change of shape upon reversal is very dramatic, and happens every time with all observers.

The cube seen projected as a perspective projection on the screen looks distorted. One face is seen as smaller than its opposite face. The smaller face is seen as the back of the cube, but at the same time it is seen as lying on the screen, at the same distance as the larger (front) face. Depth is paradoxical: both as a cube and a flat line figure on the screen. When it reverses it does not change shape, as does the object viewed directly.

What the spectator sees

What the spectator sees

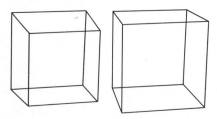
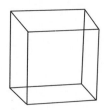

Normal   Reversed

Figure 31
Spectator using one eye

Figure 32
Spectator using one eye

Mono-zero-perspective
Object perception

Mono-zero-perspective
Picture perception

Here we replace the wire cube with a topless (truncated) pyramid. It is viewed from the smaller end, at such a distance that the *retinal image* of the nearer face is the same size as the further face. (This is done by making the front face exactly overlap the back face. The object is then rotated slightly to prevent the back being hidden by the front.) It is viewed with one eye.

It does not look like a cube. The further face looks larger than the nearer face.

When it reverses, the *apparently* further face still looks larger than the *apparently* nearer face.

So it looks like a topless pyramid, but the further face always looks the larger, whichever this may be, as it reverses in apparent depth.

This is a Necker cube. No face is indicated by perspective as the back or the front. They look the same size, and there is no size change upon reversal. (But see later comments on the importance of the texture of the screen.) Depth is paradoxical.

What the spectator sees

What the spectator sees

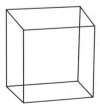

Normal   Reversed

47

Figure 33

Spectator using two eyes

Figure 34

Spectator using two eyes

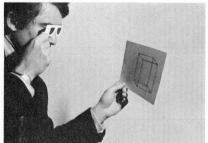

Stereo-perspective
Object perception

Here we look at the wire cube with *both* eyes.
It looks like a cube; all sides of equal length
and all angles right angles, though as for the
single-eyed view the image of the back face is
physically smaller than the image of the front.
It seldom reverses in depth, though it *can*
reverse. When reversed it is curiously
puzzling, not looking quite real. We will have
more to say about this effect later.
When it does reverse in depth, it looks
distorted, no longer like a cube; as in the one
eye's view the apparent back looks too large.

Stereo-perspective
Picture perception

We see the picture as three-dimensional,
looking incredibly real. It may indeed be
impossible to tell it from the same object (the
wire cube) seen directly.
It looks like a true cube, with no distortion.
When reversed (which rarely happens) the
stereo picture cube looks distorted, just as
for direct viewing of the cube object.
If the eyes are switched over: the stereo
picture cube looks larger when behind the
screen – i.e. when apparently more distant
from the observer.

What the spectator sees

What the spectator sees

Figure 35

Spectator using two eyes

Figure 36

Spectator using two eyes

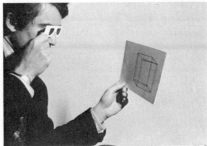

**Stereo-zero-perspective
Object perception**

Here we look again at our topless pyramid, but with both eyes. It looks, correctly, like a topless pyramid. The nearer face looks smaller than the front face as it physically is, though both faces give the same-sized images to the eyes.
When reversed (rare) the apparent back looks too large.

**Stereo-zero-perspective
Picture perception**

The back and front are physically the same size on the screen, but they do not look the same size: the apparent back looks larger. When reversed (rare) the apparent back also looks larger: but when this reversal takes place it has a curious unreal appearance.

What the spectator sees

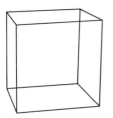

What the spectator sees

We may now summarise the main findings into a table, showing what happens for each of the four projections, both when the figure is seen correctly, in the sense that it is not reversed in depth, and when it is depth-reversed.

Conditions giving distortion (yes) and no distortion (no)

When seen correctly in depth				
	Mono-perspective	Mono-zero-perspective	Stereo perspective	Stereo-zero-perspective
Object	no	yes	no	no (usually)
Picture	no? (paradoxical)	yes (paradoxical)	no	yes

When perceptually depth-reversed				
	Mono-perspective	Mono-zero-perspective	Stereo perspective	Stereo-zero-perspective
Object	yes	yes	yes (rare)	yes (rare)
Picture	yes? (paradoxical)	yes (paradoxical)	yes (rare)	yes (rare)

By 'distorted', we mean that it does not look like a cube object. By 'paradoxical' we mean that the depth of the figure is confounded by the picture's background: it is seen to lie both on its background and in the quasi-depth of one-eyed picture space. (This paradox of depth does not occur for direct vision of objects, or for stereo picture vision.)

What do these experiments tell us about perception? Among other things, they tell us that seeing pictures is very different from seeing normal objects. This means that pictures are *not* typical objects for the eye, and must be treated as a very special case. But, as we started out by saying, most experiments on perception have used pictures. If nothing else, we have learned that we must be careful in assessing their significance – particularly careful over assuming that what these experiments show is applicable directly to the perceptions of normal objects.

Our experiments also show that pictures can be quite surprisingly inadequate for giving perception even of familiar objects.

Paradoxical figures
Pictures are objects in their own right – flat patterns of light and shade and colour – while at the same time they are seen as entirely different objects in a different space. But no object can be in two places at the same time, or be more than one size or shape; and yet an object *as seen in a*

picture is in a different place, is a different size, and has the added dimension of depth.

All pictures are paradoxical – in the sense that they have visually this extraordinary double reality: flat objects seen as flat, and at the same time as quite different three-dimensional objects in a different space. This double reality is an essential paradox of all pictures.

Artists are free to draw any visual world they choose. Unlike a camera, artists are not limited to varieties of geometrical perspective but can, if they wish, represent

37. Engraving by William Hogarth of a fisherman (1754). Hogarth combines various views and perspectives to produce an impossible picture.

51

38. Engraving by the Dutch artist, M.C.Escher, of a waterfall, apparently running continuously uphill.

distant objects the same size or larger than nearer objects of the same size. They can introduce all manner of distortions, make distant objects partly hide nearer ones, and generally rewrite the Universe.

Not only can artists make the picture plane appear largely three-dimensional, but the reverse is also possible: three-dimensional shapes can be made to look flat – or some other shape – with suitable painted shadows or other deliberately misleading 'cues' to distance.

Hogarth deliberately misused perspective in his engraving of a fisherman (figure 37). At first sight this looks like a normal, sensible picture, but a closer look shows that the actual scene could not appear as shown in the engraving. There are several visual paradoxes, all concerned

39. Engraving by Escher showing
an impossible house.

with where the various objects, the fisherman's rod and
line, the bridge and so on, lie in the third dimension of
depth. Hogarth engraved this picture to illustrate principles of perspective, quite rightly drawing attention to its
power by deliberate misuse.

More recently, the Dutch artist Escher has produced
many fascinating engravings showing paradoxes of depth.
He shows a waterfall continually running uphill (figure
38), and where is the ladder in figure 39? Perhaps even
more striking because simpler, are the impossible figures
of L.S. and R.Penrose. They call these 'impossible objects',
but this is unfortunate for it is possible to make actual
objects, not only pictures, which appear impossible. I shall
call them 'impossible figures' for this reason, reserving

'impossible objects' for actual objects which may appear paradoxical.

The 'impossible triangle' figure is particularly striking. At first it may look like a normal triangle, but it is not. Each corner looks perfectly possible by itself, but surely no actual object could have corners presenting these angles of view to the observer? Each corner is shown from a different angle of view; surely this is impossible? The perceptual mind boggles at the thought that this drawing could represent an actual object, as we would see it directly with the eye.

40. The impossible triangle of L.S. and R.Penrose. Could it exist, as an object?

In fact – and this may be quite surprising – it *is* possible to construct an object which appears just like this drawing.

Figure 41 is a photograph of just such an object. This is in no way a trick photograph, though the camera position is carefully chosen. The object is made of wood, and it is not painted with shadow or any kind of misleading information. The way it is lit for the photograph is not critical. This object exists. To the naked eye it appears from this same view point just as it does in the photograph.

41. This is an untouched photograph of an object which – *although it exists* – appears impossible.

42–4. Photographs of the object shown in figure 41 from different view points. Now its true shape is seen. It still appears paradoxical when viewed from the one critical position, although we know the truth about its shape. The implications about our beliefs are frightening!

Even when we know the answer – that it is not really a triangle but a quite different three-dimensional object – it is extremely difficult to see correctly.

If we are right in saying that perception is a matter of selecting appropriate hypotheses of external objects, according to prevailing information, then we can explain the difficulty we have in seeing this object correctly. The true solution – the rather queer-shaped three-dimensional wooden object – is an extremely unlikely solution to the problem: what object does this retinal image represent? To get the right answer requires an imaginative leap. The retinal image gives no hint that the object is three-dimensional; yet only by accepting that it is can the three views of the corners be reconciled into a single possible object.

It is particularly interesting that we can know the solution intellectually – we can even make the object and study it from all points of view – and still not see it, from the critical position, correctly. The correct solution is evidently so unlikely that an appropriate object-hypothesis is never selected. Though visual perception involves problem-solving, evidently it does not follow that when we know the solution intellectually we will necessarily see it correctly. This is a conclusion of theoretical and practical importance.

Another now well-known impossible figure is the three prongs of figure 45. What happens to the middle prong? Is there a middle prong? If so, does it follow the same position in depth as the outer two, or does it dip down below them? It seems, in a curious way, to do both at the same time. But that is impossible for one object, or one part of an object cannot exist in two places at the same time. The middle prong cannot both be at the *same* depth

45. The impossible prongs. The middle prong appears in two places at the same time. Strictly, it cannot be perceived. It calls up no acceptable perceptual hypothesis; and there seems to be no three-dimensional object which resolves this paradox.

as the outer two and *below* them, and yet according to the lines of the drawing it is in both places at once. We can adopt no perceptual hypothesis for reconciling these features of the drawing into a possible object, and so no possible object-hypothesis is selected by the retinal image given by this drawing, and we *cannot see it*. In this case the various parts cannot be reconciled even by adopting a highly unlikely hypothesis. The central prong is directly indicated as being in two places at once. If no hypothesis will reconcile the elements, no corresponding actual object can be made – so this is different from the triangle.

The artist is free to combine any visual features he likes into a picture, and so he may create a paradox which cannot be resolved. The fact that the impossible triangle can be made shows that this does have a solution, in terms of the world of objects, though the visual system cannot discover it. This raises the questions: Why are some shapes so difficult? Do they violate rules of some kind, or are they simply too unusual?

The design of the impossible triangle object is shown in figures 42–4. It is worth making, and looking at, an actual object such as this one which looks impossible. Although the retinal image of the model is the same as the photograph we know that it is a solid object. We see that it is made of wood, of square cross-section. Although the wood looks, and is, real, still we cannot find a perceptual solution to the problem of how the pieces of wood lie in space. To see solid pieces of wood forming an impossible though simple object, a paradox in space, is a remarkable experience, surely more interesting than a fleeting 'trick of the light', or a conjuring trick which deceives the eye by quickness of the hand.

The fact that a three-dimensional object can be visually paradoxical shows that what we called the 'essential paradox' of pictures is not the only kind of visual paradox. This object shows that we can get depth paradoxes apart from the picture-plane paradox – for here there is no picture plane.

This object is paradoxical when we do not have the correct visual hypothesis for interpreting the shape at the retina. In particular, when we see it as two-dimensional, though in fact it is a three-dimensional object, then the various parts appear paradoxically related.

Pictures can be depth-paradoxical apart from the picture plane: (a) when they are wrongly interpreted spatially though they *could* be correctly interpreted by finding a better object-hypothesis, or (b) when essentially incompatible depth features are presented. In this case, no consistent interpretation is possible.

We find, then, the following kinds of picture paradoxes: *First:* All pictures are paradoxical in being physically patterns of marks on a flat sheet, but visually both flat objects and three-dimensional objects in a quite different space. This is the essential double-reality of pictures, which makes them unique as visual objects of perception. *Second:* Pictures can present mutually incompatible depth-features. These would be paradoxical even with no hint of a background. Since the artist is free to present any depth-features he wishes in a picture, he can produce a great variety of paradoxes of this kind. But this cannot occur in objects.

Third: Pictures can appear paradoxical when the observer happens or is led to select an inappropriate 'object-hypothesis' for interpreting – seeing – the picture in terms of normal objects.

We know from the model 'impossible triangle' that this kind of depth-paradox is not limited to pictures but can occur with true three-dimensional objects, viewed from certain critical positions.

There are other kinds of paradoxes in pictures besides depth-paradoxes. A painting of a ship does not have to be full-sized for the painting to be *seen* as a full-sized ship. When it (or a model) is seen as both its true size and as a full-sized ship, it is perceptually paradoxical.

We may say that for a picture to be paradoxical, rather than merely unusual, it must present incompatible *spatial* information. All manner of features of different objects can be combined in one space and we may get a composite object which as a matter of contingent fact could not – or would be most unlikely to – exist as an object, but they are not *logically* impossible (figure 46). Similarly in speech: 'This blonde brunette' is paradoxical, but 'This glass mountain' is merely unlikely, or contingently impossible.

Some paradoxes can be resolved, others not. When a paradox is due to specifically given incompatible information it is not possible to resolve it – without rejection of information. But this does not truly resolve the paradox; it changes the problem.

Paradoxes which can be resolved are those which are due to an inappropriate hypothesis adopted for reconciling the given elements. In the impossible object, if we can see it as its true three-dimensional shape – actually quite unlike the triangular image it gives from the critical position – then the paradox disappears. We then see that this image is a special case, subsumed under the general perceptual hypothesis of the shape of the object, which holds for *any* viewing position. The nearest we ever get to the 'truth' is a hypothesis which, when accepted, gives no surprises in new situations. We begin, surely, to see that the use of the word 'paradox' for pictures is no idle pun based on its more usual use for arguments and scientific enquiry. Perceiving is a kind of thinking. We have examples of ambiguities, paradoxes, distortions and uncertainties in perception as in all other thinking. They bedevil the intelligent eye as they are the causes and the symptoms of error in the most concrete and the most abstract thought.

46. This drawing does not combine *logically incompatible* elements, but they are together most *improbable*. Tree-people do not exist, and our knowledge of objects is challenged by the notion. We can 'read' parts as a hand *and* a branch; a finger *and* a twig. This picture plays explicitly with our repertoire of stored object-hypotheses. (After Hieronymus Bosch.)

We can see these signs and symptoms of error in perception – paradox, ambiguity, uncertainty and distortion – as clues to the ways the brain uses sensory information to jump from the patterns of sensory information to the so-different perceptions of objects. When it leaps wrongly, to land in error, we can learn from the pitfalls the strategy it adopts. From our eyes' errors we can look behind the eyes and see something of the most extraordinary and the most complicated functioning system on Earth, to discover at least in outline how it solves problems far too difficult for any computer so far conceived, every time we see an object – or a picture.

Uncertain figures

The conclusion so far is that pictures are not very satisfactory for representing the structure of three-dimensional objects – unless we introduce the second eye to give stereo vision.

So far we have only looked at one object directly and in various projections – a wire cube. This was convenient for estimating gross distortions, for it is very easy to judge the equality of the various parts of a simple regular figure and so to know by direct observation whether and how it is distorted. What happens, though, if we take not a regular figure such as a cube but some unfamiliar or random figure – such as the branch of a tree? This could have almost any shape; for though we may recognise it as part of a tree every individual tree is unique in its detailed structure, and so we cannot already know or guess the shape of this particular tree.

We need an experimental technique for establishing the accuracy of perception for various picture projections of random and unfamiliar objects. How can we do it? We might, somehow, try to present the structure in such a way that perceptual errors become obvious and can be described. We will adopt a method.

We have argued that to see correctly is to select an object-hypothesis, which not only fits current facts but also is predictive. To describe perception as selecting 'object-hypotheses' is no vague analogy to the use of the word 'hypothesis' in science. A scientific hypothesis must be capable of predicting future events for it to have any power. The same should be true of perceptual object-hypotheses; it is indeed their ability to predict which gives power over enemies and over nature. Prediction makes it possible to plan action before events.

We can use the essential predictive power of object-hypotheses to check, experimentally, their accuracy. If they fail to predict the stages of a regular repeated set of events then the prevailing hypothesis must be in error. It will be in error just where it fails to predict. And so we should be able to use success or failure at prediction as a sign of the appropriateness of perceptual object-hypotheses.

Now how can we use this idea? Can we devise a simple situation for revealing failures of perceptual prediction?

We shall be concerned only with a certain kind of predictive failure. Consider the case of a plane projection – a flat picture. If this is interpreted – seen – correctly in terms of the true three-dimensional structure of the object, then we should be able to *predict the projection from a new point of view*. This gives us a clue for devising a method for testing the predictive power of object-hypotheses.

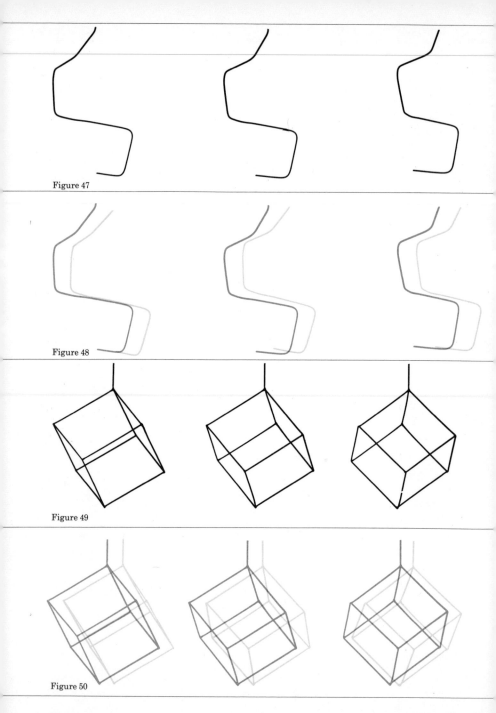

Figure 47

Figure 48

Figure 49

Figure 50

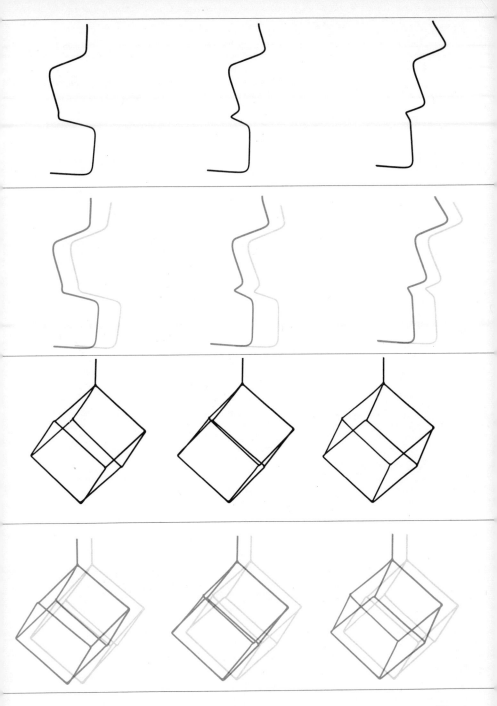

If a new view of an object is surprising, then the related object-hypothesis must be incomplete or in error.

If we allow appreciable time to elapse between an initial and a different, second view, surprise at the second view could be due to a distortion in memory, occurring between the two views. We must therefore avoid delay between presentations. Also, the surprise – the difference between the first and second perceptions of the object as a three-dimensional structure – must be clear to the observer.

We start, then, with a projection of a three-dimensional object. We can use our shadow-projection technique for this. Now, suppose we *continuously rotate* the object. This will give an ever-changing, but repeating, flat projection of the object.

If the perception of the object given by its projection is correct, we should see the changing projections as an unchanging object. But if the shape of the object, as seen from its projections, *changes* – then the perception must be *wrong* at least for some of the projections.

Using the shadow projector, we suspend our object (the cube, part of a tree, a crystal structure, a bent piece of wire – any skeleton object) from a small synchronous motor, to give it slow continuous rotation. We then watch the shadow projection on the screen, the object itself being hidden from direct view by the screen as before. What happens?

An unfamiliar object, say a bent piece of wire, gives a most curious and interesting effect. For a time it may look simply like a shape rotating, all the parts rotating at the same speed and in the same direction. It looks what it is – a rigid bent wire slowly rotating. But then, quite suddenly, it will utterly change: parts of the wire will take on a 'life of their own'. Parts will speed up or slow down; bends will change their angle, like limbs slowly writhing – it is no longer a rigid dead shape but a thing come alive full of relative movement (figure 47).

When a bend in the wire is seen as a changing angle – rather than rotating as part of a rigid object – we know that the projection has been interpreted wrongly. Only when it is seen correctly – when the object-hypothesis fits the object – will it be seen as an unchanging, simply rotating structure. Stereo vision gives the same effect – the unfamiliar object is now seen unchanging as it rotates. Something of this may be seen from figure 48, by wearing the coloured spectacles.

Taking the wire cube as a familiar and simple geometrical figure; we find that it continues to be perceived as a rigid object as it rotates, though only a flat projection is presented to one eye (figure 49). It does, however, spontaneously reverse in depth; and with each depth-reversal the apparent direction of rotation reverses, as we should expect. There is no available sensory information for setting the depth-orientation – any more than there is for a Necker cube drawn on paper – and the apparent rotation is geared to the prevailing depth-hypothesis, changing with it. *These* ambiguities are removed by stereo vision (figure 50).

Now what happens if we remove parts of the cube, leaving, say, one face and a few edges; or part of a face, say a single right angle? By discovering how much of the original object must be retained to maintain a stable perception – by allowing prediction to new view points – we should be able to establish at least some of the basic units of object-hypotheses, to discover building blocks of perception.

Here are some results which seem to apply to virtually all adult observers; at any rate to all who are from our culture, and so familiar with cubes, etc.

Cube with two edges removed (figures 51 and 52)
This still appears as an unchanging cube-like solid object. Evidently this selects the object-hypothesis of a cube. Adding stereo has little effect, except largely to prevent depth reversals, with associated changes in direction of apparent rotation.

Two opposed faces, joined by one edge (figures 53 and 54)
This is quite fascinating: the two squares remain squares, but they no longer remain parallel, facing each other. They rotate separately, from their points of suspension from the linking edge, either in the same direction or in opposite directions at the same time. Further, they can appear to remain normal to the observer but to slide across each other, as the figure in fact rotates as a whole. Evidently the cube-hypothesis has now been abandoned.

The addition of stereo to this figure removes these alternative interpretations and we now see an unchanging rotating object – two parallel squares joined by an edge – as parts of a cube.

One face with a single edge (figures 55 and 56)
The face remains a square, but the edge 'takes off on its own', seldom remaining at right angles to the rotating square. Evidently the cube-hypothesis is now totally abandoned but we are left with the hypothesis that this is a (rotating) square. The edge in fact fixed to it is no part of this hypothesis, for it is seen to move quite independently of the square. This shows that no assumption of the angle of the edge to the square (actually a right angle) has been accepted.

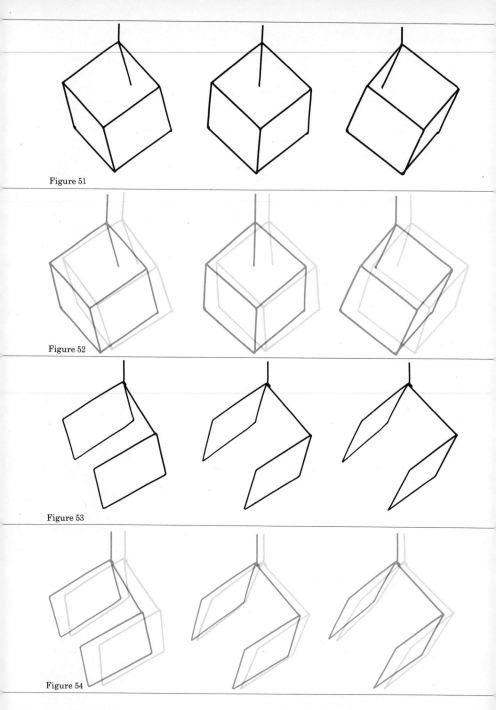

Figure 51

Figure 52

Figure 53

Figure 54

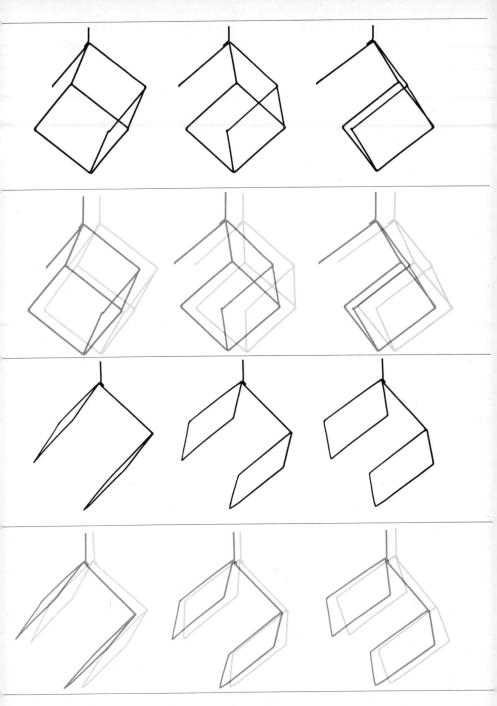

Adding stereo fixes the edge to the square so that now it is seen to rotate as one rigid object.

Part of a face (figures 57 and 58)
When we remove part of the square, to leave a single right angle, we find that the square-hypothesis is lost. It changes dramatically while rotating, switching systematically between two quite different perceptual hypotheses, neither of which is in fact correct. While the wire object is nearly normal to the screen, it is not seen to rotate; but to open and close, like a pair of scissors. When nearly closed, it suddenly starts to rotate; remaining at a fixed angle of considerably less (about 30°) than its true angle (90°).

Adding stereo removes these two (false) perceptual hypotheses and we see the figure correctly, the angle and the speed of rotation remaining unchanged. This is a somewhat surprising result, for although right angles seem to be accepted as a basis of size scaling (page 79) nevertheless they do not seem to be a basic unit of object-hypotheses, as judged with this technique.

This is but a start to trying to establish characteristics of object-hypotheses by using their essential predictive power as an index of the 'units' that form them. We would like to know in detail the developmental stages by which they are formed through childhood, the effects of cultural differences and above all how the 'units' are selected and assembled to give perception. But perhaps this brief description of just one experimental situation is sufficient to show that we have a technique which though simple may prove surprisingly powerful for studying a fundamental problem for the intelligent eye – the assumptions it accepts for perceiving the world of objects from the fleeting, tenuous, optical patterns.

Adding the second eye
When we add the second eye to give stereoscopic vision, (by introducing the second point-source light, page 44) we find that almost all objects are seen without these internal changes as they rotate. The added stereo depth information serves to solve the perceptual space problem in nearly all cases. The simple cube can, however, sometimes reverse with the stereoscopic projection, or when seen directly with both eyes. Also, a figure having marked but misleading depth-features, such as converging lines accepted as perspective, can be seen incorrectly in stereo-projection. It is sometimes thought that stereo information settles any question of three-dimensional structure, but this is not correct. Marked perspective can dominate, and spontaneous reversals of depth-ambiguous figures can occasionally still take place.

Stereo-given depth is totally rejected when the resulting perception would be sufficiently bizarre. A dramatic example is an inside-out head – such as the inside of a cast, or the back of a mask. Such inside-out faces are rejected: the cast is seen as a normal face, though in fact it is inside-out (figure 117). It seems that stereo vision, though giving non-ambiguous depth information, nevertheless is not accepted as a final arbiter of structure. It does resolve ambiguities and uncertainties in unfamiliar figures – which have no object-hypotheses for selection – but it is not accepted against high probabilities of alternative hypotheses being appropriate.

It is important to note that object-hypotheses cannot include information of the particular distance, orientation, motion or generally the size of the observed object. (Except for special cases – such as the moon – which always present the same aspect to the observer – except indeed to astronauts.) Our main thesis is that the various depth cues, including stereo information, are used to set these parameters; using real-time visual data since the information is not internally available in the stored perceptual hypotheses. But when real-time sensory data are incompatible with a firmly held hypothesis the data may be rejected. This shows the power of perceptual 'prejudice' against available 'facts'. But since available data are always liable to error, the preference for stored data based on the past may generally lead to greater reliability, provided it is appropriate. It is an old joke among scientists: 'Don't bother me with facts, they might upset my theory.' In science and in perception this can sometimes be a good initial strategy – for data can be uncertain and facts can be misinterpreted.

It is particularly interesting that we accept plane projections (including retinal images) as representing an object though in fact *the selected object-hypothesis is imprecise*. For example, looking at a tree we see that it is a tree, though at the same time we cannot say which branch lies in front, which behind another (figure 59). The structure is not in detail represented in the brain, though it is correctly classified as a tree. A plane projection is sufficient for selecting the hypothesis that it is a tree, and even what kind of tree, but the structure of a particular tree cannot be included in the general perceptual hypothesis. We do not need stereo vision for classifying the tree, though it is most useful for climbing it (figure 60). We may think we see an object or picture in precise spatial detail but this feeling of precision can be most misleading, for it may be based on arbitrary assumptions.

It is often important to have precise perception of

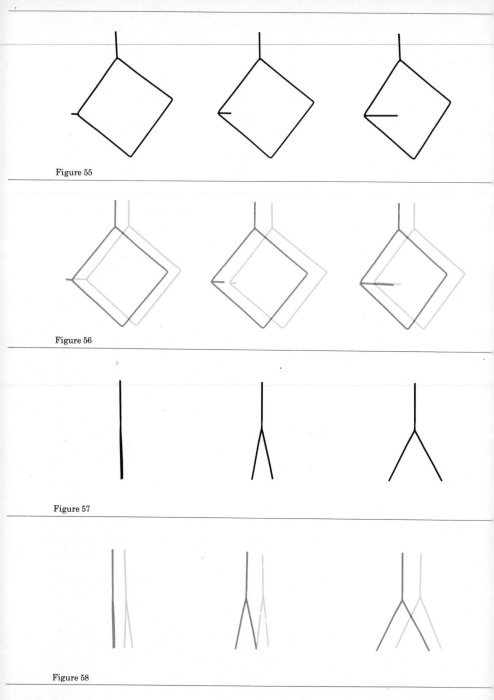

Figure 55

Figure 56

Figure 57

Figure 58

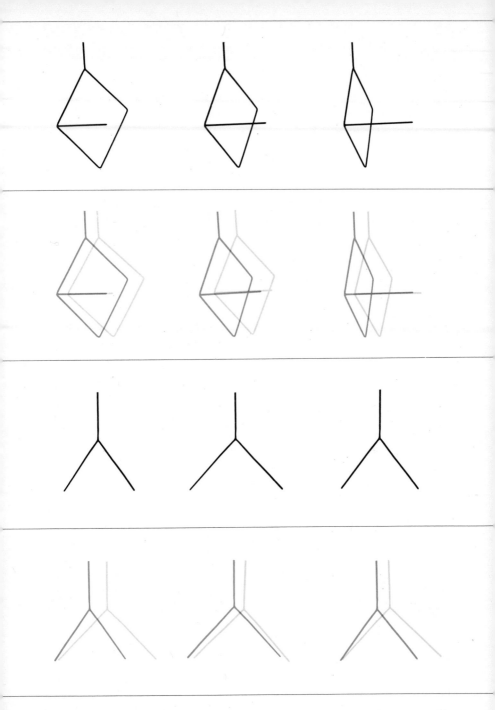

59. This is immediately recognised as part of a tree. But can we see how its parts lie in depth? Just how the twigs and branches lie is uncertain. We accept that it is a tree, without being able to specify its precise form. This is adequate for recognition but not for climbing it. For objects such as trees which can have a large variety of shapes, stereoscopic vision is most important for resolving the ambiguities. Each particular shape cannot be stored as an object-hypothesis; unless indeed it is a particular, well-known tree.

spatial relationships. It is also important, especially in technology, to be able to represent structures accurately in pictures or in some other way. We have found that stereo vision can be of great help, especially where the details of the structure are not stored in the selected object-hypothesis. Why should we not add stereo vision to pictures? Why not draw in 3-D? We will discuss this possibility later (page 133). Meanwhile, we will consider another kind of error in the perception of certain pictures and objects – distortions. It turns out that these will lead us directly to some quite complicated issues, so we must spend some time on why visual perceptions should be distorted in certain familiar and often apparently simple situations.

60. Viewing this with the stereo glasses, we see the shape un-ambiguously. We could climb it, though we have never seen this particular tree before. Normal pictures or single retinal images are inadequate for such objects, which demand the non-ambiguous information of stereo vision for more than classification into a class of objects.

4

We have seen that pictures and objects – as well as statements made with words in a language – can be paradoxical, ambiguous or uncertain. They can also appear distorted.

Visual distortions are often simply called 'illusions', but of course there are many other kinds of illusions. There can also be distortions of various kinds in the other senses: temperature, taste, the loudness or pitch of sound, the brightness or colour of light and the speed at which objects appear to move.

Some distortions are due to the sensory receptors becoming fatigued, or 'adapted', by prolonged or intense stimulation. This can happen for any of the senses and quite large distortions can result. Here are some ways of adapting the senses to give distortions:

1 *Weight*
After carrying a heavy weight for a few minutes, the arm feels light and may involuntarily rise up several inches.

2 *Temperature*
This is an ancient experiment, and worth trying. Put one hand in a bowl of hot water, the other in a bowl of cold water. After a few minutes or so put both hands in a bowl of tepid water. Although both hands are now in water of the same temperature, the one that was in hot water feels it as cold while the other feels it as hot – one hand

61 and 62. One hand is placed in a bowl of cold water, the other in hot. If the hands are then placed together in a bowl of tepid water (figure 62) the water feels, and is judged to be, at the same time warm for one hand and cool for the other. The cold and hot water have selectively adapted the hands, upsetting their calibration, so that temperature is then judged incorrectly by each of them. Although we know intellectually that water cannot be both hot and cold at the same time, this is how we feel and judge it to be. The brain does not reject the paradox. We experience something we know to be physically impossible.

feels the same water as cold, the other as hot. It is interesting that if a hand is placed in water which is heated (or cooled) so slowly that the change of temperature is not felt, the hand still adapts to the changed temperature – distortion occurs though the adaptation is not experienced.

3 *Taste*
Sweet drinks taste gradually less sweet. Try keeping a strong solution of water and sugar in the mouth for a few seconds and then taste fresh water. It will now taste distinctly salty.

4 *Loudness and pitch*
Adaptations to loudness or pitch of sound can be dangerous, but are easy to demonstrate in the laboratory.

5 *Velocity*
Distortion of apparent speed is common while driving: a car moving at 30 m.p.h. seems almost ridiculously slow after half an hour's continuous driving on a motorway.

As in other adaptations, reversal can also occur: if you watch the spiral in figure 63 rotating on a record-player turntable for a few seconds, it will appear to expand while rotating and to shrink after adaptation.

6 *Brightness*
Adaptation to local regions of bright light give the well-known visual after-images: bright, dark or coloured. If a lamp is looked at (with the eyes moving as little as possible) for several seconds, when the eyes are transferred to a white wall or sheet of paper, the effect of adaptation to white and to black will be seen quite dramatically. Adaptation to the bright light will produce a corresponding dark area, (moving with the eyes) on the grey field.

These after-image brightness and colour effects are fairly completely understood. Fixation of the red bird in figure 64 reduces the sensitivity of the retinal light receptors on which this area falls. The effect is more dramatic with a light. When the eyes are then directed to an evenly lit surface, we see the region corresponding to the part of the retina which has lost sensitivity by being exposed to bright light as darker, simply because it now transmits less signal to the brain. The frequency of nerve impulses from this region is reduced, just as when in fact we look at a darker region or object. The colour effects are similar in origin. Colour is transmitted to the brain from the retina along (almost certainly) only three channels. There are three types of ('cone') receptor, each sensitive to red, green or blue. White light activates

63. If a larger version of this spiral (as on page 189) is rotated on the turntable of a record-player, it will be seen to expand when rotated clockwise. After being viewed for several seconds and then stopped, it will appear to shrink. This is an adaptation to movement. The effect is paradoxical, for although it is seen as shrinking it is also seen to remain the same size. The after-effect of movement can be transferred to other objects.

all three colour channels, and the proportion of activity from each 'means' white. Red light gives relatively more activity in the 'red' channel, green in the 'green' channel and blue in the 'blue' channel. All colours are given by the proportional activity in the three colour channels. The visual three-channel system allows colour photography and colour TV to work by providing only three colours to the eye, these roughly matching the colour response characteristics of the three retinal colour systems. Now when one or more of the retinal colour systems has been adapted – to lose sensitivity by prolonged exposure to coloured light – the brain receives the same signal that it receives with light of the *complementary colour* of the adapting light. And so we see the complementary colour.

It is possible to impress detailed photographic-like after-images upon the retina, with a powerful electronic flash, with dramatic effect. If a darkened room is lit with a flash, it appears for several seconds in every detail so vividly that the after-image may be mistaken for the room itself, until the eyes move or it fades away.

64. Adaptation to patterns of intensity at the retina can give after-images which may be very vivid, and may be confused with objects. In this case, staring at the red bird and then looking at the centre of the bird-cage, we may see an illusory green bird in the cage. On a white background, after-images have the complementary colour of the stimulus light.
Using the coloured glasses at the end of the book, the reader may experiment with various colours of after-image, by looking at a light bulb through the glasses and transferring the gaze to white or coloured surfaces. After-images appear *larger* the more *distant* the screen on which they appear to lie. They (nearly) double in size with each doubling of distance. This is Emmert's Law. (Cf. page 92.)

76

These after-image effects are known to be at least mainly due to retinal changes in sensitivity, though there may also be some changes in the brain's projection areas with prolonged or violent stimulation of the eye. A more complicated effect, which is also probably retinal in origin, is the production of colour with flickering white light.

If the disk (figure 65) on page 191 of this book is cut out and rotated on a record-player turntable, it will gradually become coloured. The colours will vary with the speed of rotation. This is known as 'Benham's top'. It was originally produced with a black-and-white spinning top. The explanation is, almost certainly, that the three retinal colour systems have (in electronic terminology) different time-constants. The rotating disk gives intermittent stimulation to the colour receptors. It is probable that the red-, green- and blue-sensitive receptors have somewhat different time-constants, so that repeated flashes of light build up different levels of activity in the three systems – which is equivalent to a coloured light to the brain. The signals from the eye are identical and so the illusion of colour is compelling. A loss of colour balance also occurs on the screen of a colour TV receiver when the Benham's top disk is shown to the camera. The colour changes are at least as vivid as when the disk is viewed directly and are due to both the TV and the eye being affected – for the same physical reason.

65. This disk, although black and white, will appear variously coloured if rotated. Use the larger disk on page 191 on a record-player turntable. The colour signalling system of the retina is upset by the time-spaced pulses of black and white. Any colour can be generated. If the rotating disk is viewed through the red or green celluloid of the glasses, other colours may appear.

These distortions are all (with the possible exception of the movement effects) due to adaptation of peripheral sense organs. We may say that these distortions are all due to *loss of calibration of the sensory transducers*. In so far as the brain receiving the information is concerned, this is the same as the photographer whose exposure meter has been left in the sun to lose sensitivity, or the engineer whose ruler has expanded in the heat. When transducers or measuring instruments are upset, to give a different output for the same input, scale errors inevitably occur. Unless, indeed, correction is made from other information used as a check, or when the signalled information is too improbable to be accepted at face value. We may think of these adaptations as *loss of calibration* of the monitoring receptors.

Adaptation of one sensory channel, but not of another which parallels it, can lead to most curious effects. For example, the after-effect of movement given by the rotating spiral (figure 63) is paradoxical; for we see movement (expansion) – in the direction opposite to the adapting stimulation – in the after-effect, while at the same time we see that the spiral (or other object) viewed during the after-effect does not change in size. To expand

and yet not to change in size is impossible for any physical object; and so it is paradoxical. Yet this is what we see with this adaptation-illusion.

We can imagine something similar with the instruments of a car. The speed of a car can be obtained, either by noting the distance travelled over a given time, or by getting a direct velocity reading from the speedometer. Now imagine using both methods, and suppose that either the speedometer or the mileometer is in error. We would apparently receive the information that we were travelling at two different speeds at the same time; or if the speedometer had simply ceased to work, that we were both stationary and moving. No doubt we would assume that one of the instruments was incorrect rather than believe that we were travelling at two different speeds, or both stationary and moving, but the brain does not always do the same with sensory information. Sometimes information from parallel channels is accepted though they disagree. This generates not only distortion, but also paradox. We begin to see the limits of the unaided brain as an 'internal scientist', making sense of sensory data.

Paradoxes of this kind occur only when there are alternative parallel systems for signalling information. The case of colour is an example of where there is but one channel – consisting of the three kinds of receptor whose relative outputs signal colour. In this case adaptation produces a colour change but never a paradox. We cannot see an object as 'red and green all over', not because objects never are red and green all over (as some philosophers have suggested) but because the eye has but one way of signalling colour to the brain.

These distortion effects are all peripheral, due to change of sensitivity of the sensory receptors – the transducers converting certain physical events in the external world to neural signals. Sensory adaptation is so easy to produce, and can cause such compelling and potentially disturbing distortions of perception, that one is led to ask whether the lability of the sensory transducers is, so to say, a weakness of the physiological design or whether there is some good reason for their ready adaptation though the physical input has not changed. Pain receptors are relatively free of adaptation – hence persistent toothache! – which leads to the possibility that there is a 'design reason' for adaptation of this kind in other senses. A possibility, to take an analogy from instrument engineering, is that this is a safeguard against more persistent errors, through the inevitable drift that occurs in any transducer system if it is to give constant responses to steady signals – that is, if it is DC coupled. Electronic devices are very prone to this trouble. Where possible, *overleaf:*

66 and 67. A pair of Muller-Lyer 'arrow' illusion figures. The vertical lines (or separation of the 'fins') are actually the same length, but the outward-going fins increase the separation between them, while the in-going fins reduce it. This illusion is unusual in that the figure distorts itself; in most illusions a background distorts superimposed lines or other features.

68 and 69. The same distortion is produced by pictures or photographs of scenes having marked perspective. Since the world of objects is three-dimensional – and in pictures the three dimensions are compressed into two but still read by the brain in terms of the normal three-dimensional world – it is surely not surprising that there should be some systematic distortions of this kind. It is important to note that the distortions still occur when the pictures are seen as flat objects. This has important implications for an adequate theory of distortion illusions, for we cannot suppose that the size-change is due simply to apparent distance, as in the reversing cube-object experiments. We suppose that Constancy Scaling can be set directly by typical depth-features, such as perspective, even when depth is not seen, because it is countermanded for example by the texture of the picture-plane. Typical depth-features set the calibration of the visual system; but in an *atypical* situation the calibration is *inappropriate* – producing systematic distortions.

70 and 71. Muller-Lyer illusion figures, but with the separation between the fins adjusted to compensate the distortion given by the fins. This gives one way of measuring the distortion.

72. The ruler is distorted in length by the illusion figure. It is still usable provided it is in close contact with the figure.

73. A bent ruler is rather unlikely – and yet this is how we see it. These illusions are evidently not due to an internal probability outweighing retinal evidence, in any simple manner.

engineers use AC coupled circuits which, though they will adapt and so lose a long-maintained steady signal, will not give spurious signals by the components drifting. The signalling of pain is a matter of pain or no-pain. For such switched signals, AC coupling is not so necessary.

The distortions we have looked at so far build up in time, as a result of 'adaptation' or 'fatigue' of receptor mechanisms, so that the brain receives modified signals. There are, however, very striking visual distortion effects which do not build up but are seen immediately. They are extraordinarily consistent, being very much the same every time, and much the same for almost all observers. Many of them are familiar from children's books. They are often dismissed as trivial – indeed few books on perception treat them seriously. But this is surely a mistake, for they are largely repeatable phenomena, and often in the history of science apparently trivial effects – sometimes used for toys – have turned out to be of profound interest. The systematic distortions produced by certain shapes reveal some of the most interesting processes in perception.

The distortions are of size or shape. In distortion-illusion figures, some lines appear too long or too short, others bent, while still others are displaced from their true positions. The errors can be as great as 30 per cent or even more: quite large enough to be serious in practice.

Some illusion figures are surprisingly simple, for example the most famous, the Muller-Lyer 'arrows' figure (figures 66 and 67). Here there are no 'jazzy' repeated lines, no queer unfamiliar shapes, nothing vague or half-hidden. Simply adding 'arrow heads' to a line makes the line appear shorter (with in-going arrows) or longer (with out-going arrows). Why should this be? Why should such a simple and familiar shape so upset the eye? Is it the receptors of the retina or their interconnections which are upset, or is the origin of the distortions in the brain? Before tackling the problem, which is not easy, we will consider how the distortions can be objectively measured.

Errors of length can be measured quite accurately, using a 'neutral' comparison line adjusted in length until it has the same apparent length as the distorted line. If the neutral comparison line and the distorted feature are measured with a scale – a simple ruler – the difference given by the readings from the ruler will indicate the distortion, even though the ruler itself may appear distorted in the illusion situation. It can be distorted and yet read correctly, providing it is placed close to, or better touching, the lines to be measured. Figure 72 shows how a ruler may appear when placed on a distortion figure and nevertheless read correctly.

66

67

68

69

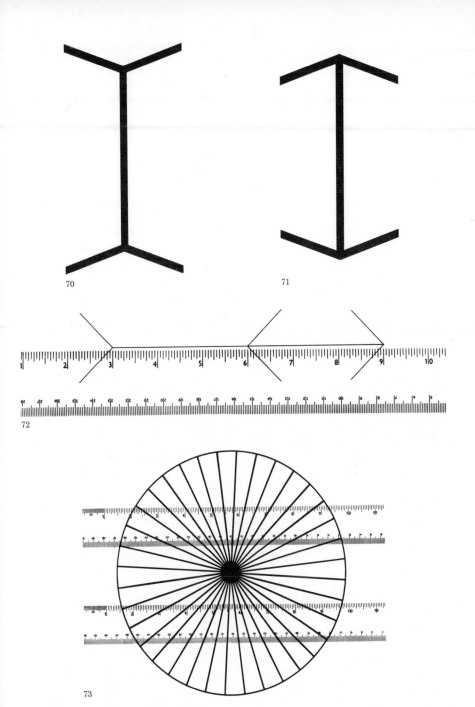

70

71

72

73

It is possible to measure some distortions by redrawing the figure to cancel the distortion. Figures 70 and 71 show the 'arrows' illusion with the figures *actually* different in size. They may look very similar but they are not, as can be checked with a ruler. This is essentially a 'null' method of measuring, and can be very useful for perceptual studies as in other scientific measurements. There is, however, a difficulty. By 'distorting' the figure, the input to the eye is no longer the same as it was. How do we know the effect of this difference on the perceptual system? It will probably be small, but this is an assumption and may have to be tested. The situation is analogous to the Heisenberg principle in physics: that the act of measuring can upset what is measured. Even the neutral line comparison method can change the situation, for the original illusion figure did not have this extra line in the field of view. This is a difficulty to bear in mind but generally it is possible to measure visual distortions in these simple ways with confidence.

Are the distortions in the eyes or in the brain?

It is often very difficult to establish just *where* in the nervous system a given function, or some temporary or permanent loss of function, is situated. The same is true in engineering systems, especially those not understood in detail. Consider plumbing; an air lock may be anywhere in a pipe. A skilled plumber may make a shrewd guess that it is in a bend rather than a straight piece of pipe and may be able to deduce, by turning on and off various taps and so on, which section of pipe is affected. To do this he will draw up (on paper or in his brain) a model of the system and consider it in terms of certain more or less general principles; for example that water flows downwards, that it finds its own level, that hot water can produce steam – perhaps to form an air lock if the thermostat is set too high or sticks. The diagnosis of plumbing faults is comparatively easy, because there are but a few things that can go wrong and there are fairly direct ways for discovering and curing the trouble: including banging suspected parts, which is not unknown for electronic engineers and neurologists!

The nervous system is so interconnected that an error in one part can affect some quite distant part, which may seem separate functionally and yet turn out to be associated in some subtle way. Even where there is a clear chain of processes along a single neural path (which is extremely rare) it is very difficult to locate a disturbance along the path. There are technical problems of recording activity within the nervous system, and there are also surprisingly difficult conceptual problems: especially when we do not know the function of each physical part of the system. The plumber has to know at least the rudiments of how thermostats, heating elements and taps work, to locate and correct even the simplest fault; but many of the basic functional processes of the nervous system remain mysterious and so it is very difficult to *locate functions*. Before they can be located they have to be defined and understood. A conceptual model of a system is vital for describing the functions of its parts. For example we can describe after-images in terms of loss of sensitivity of the retinal receptors with some confidence, because we understand the receptors' function in the visual system (to capture quanta and convert light energy into visual signals), but can we hope to understand the distortion illusions until we know the kind of functional processes responsible for perception?

It would be a help to know whether the distortions are in the eyes (or associated with their movements), or whether the errors lie in the brain. Fortunately, it is rather easy to show that the origin of the distortion illusions is, at least primarily, in the brain and not the eyes. This has been demonstrated by presenting selected parts of the figures to one eye and the remaining parts to the other eye, using a stereoscope. There are two kinds of stereoscopic experiments for this: (1) the 'test' part of the figure – the distorted part – is presented to one eye, while the 'inducing' part is presented to the other eye, or (2) the figure is broken up into random dots. *Neither* eye receives a distinguishable pattern, but by fusion in the brain of the signals from the two eyes, the pair of random dot patterns are combined to form the illusion figure. Now, if under either of these conditions the figures are seen whole, *but the distortion is absent*, then we would deduce that the origin of the distortion is localised in each eye system (probably in the retina). But if the distortion still occurs, then it must lie in the brain *after* the fusion of the information from the two eyes. The 'test' and 'inducing' parts of illusion figures have been presented separately to the two eyes by several experimenters, first by Witasek in 1899 and more recently by a Japanese worker, Ohwaki (1960) and by Springbeck (1961). They found that the distortions, though present, were greatly reduced. The problem was taken up by Boring (1961), Day (1961) and Schiller and Wiener (1962). They considered the possibility that something special to the stereoscopic situation reduced the illusions, thus questioning the direct inference that there was a large retinal component. This often happens in science: for example, we know that feathers fall slowly not because gravity is ineffective for feathers, but because air resistance slows them in spite of gravity. Air resistance can look like reduced gravity, and so experiments are needed to test between these very different hypotheses. Boring noted that the stereoscopic presentation tended to give depth-perception of the figures. Day noted that there was a lot of 'retinal rivalry' – the figures not always fusing into a single stable perception but forming ever-changing mixtures. This effect is shown in figure 74. So there were two suggested factors which might reduce the distortions. Schiller and

74. Retinal rivalry. If this is viewed with the coloured glasses, one eye will receive the red lines, the other eye the green lines. The brain fails to combine the two images continuously and we see a curious shifting, jazzing effect.

75 *opposite*. By wearing the coloured glasses, we may present parts of figures to the eyes separately. The illusions still occur, showing that the origin of the distortions is in the brain and not in the eyes. (After Schiller and Wiener, 1962.)

Wiener presented five distortion illusions (figure 75) stereoscopically under conditions designed to reduce both depth-perception and retinal rivalry. They used very short exposures for this purpose. The result was that the distortions were virtually the same as for normal viewing. It therefore seems that it is the tendency to see depth, or retinal rivalry or both, which reduces the distortions, indicating that the distortion is, after all, in the brain and not the eye.

This is confirmed by the second way of sharing the figures between the two eyes – random correlated dot patterns. This technique is recent, and is due to Bela Julesz, who has used it to brilliant effect in experiments on the nature of stereoscopic vision. It has been shown that illusions, including the Muller-Lyer figure, are seen with undiminished distortion in this situation. So we have every reason to believe that the distortions have their origin in the brain.

But finding that their origin is in the brain opens up an uncomfortably large number of possibilities. Worst of all: do we know enough about the functional processes

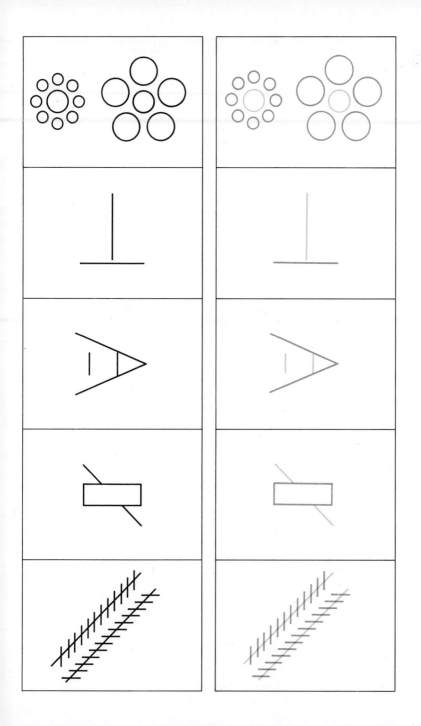

of the brain to be able to point to a process which may be upset by these shapes? Can we explain the illusions without understanding the function of the brain in great detail? Perhaps we are in the sad case of the plumber with noises in the pipes and reduced flow, who does not know about steam producing air locks, or sticking thermostats overheating the water to produce steam where no steam should be. Or like the television engineer-apprentice, who tries to explain why a picture is distorted without knowing that the picture is based on co-ordinates, set up by line and frame scans – distortion of these giving distorted pictures.

It is worth pursuing these analogy-examples a little further. Suppose the television engineer does understand the *basic principles* of picture formation, but does not know the *particular circuits* in any detail. Could he then explain – could he understand – distortion of the pictures? The answer, surely, is that he would have an explanation which would hold true for all television receivers sharing the same basic principles of operation, though he could not specify just which components are at fault or say just why a given faulty component should produce the distortion of the scan, and so the picture. His understanding would be intellectually satisfying, and a large step towards the detailed knowledge necessary to effect a cure. He would, at least, know which questions to ask. Similarly, we need understanding of the brain in terms of functional principles before we can ascribe significance to particular circuits or components. It is in these terms that we should hope to understand the illusion-distortions: more detailed knowledge must come later when the physiology is known more fully.

We may look back at how we regard perception. We regard it as making remarkably efficient use of strictly inadequate, and so ambiguous, information for selecting internally stored hypotheses of the current state of the external world. These are in terms of what kind of objects are present, and their sizes and their positions in space. Of particular importance is their distance from the observer. This is ever-changing (except for such objects as the moon, as seen from Earth) and so distance cannot be included in the object-hypotheses. It follows that each object must be placed in an appropriate position in space *according to current sensory information*. Object-recognition is simplified by the fact that most familiar objects are largely redundant. Faces have two eyes – and so but one needs to be seen. If there is an eye – there will surely also be a nose. If a head – somewhere near a body, legs and feet. Indeed we could make no sense of close-ups on the cinema screen if we did not make great use of such associated facts about familiar objects. But this redundancy of objects is not available for setting sizes and distances. A given object may have a variety of sizes, and has a very large range of possible distances. So *current sensory information must be used for setting size and distance scales.* If, for some reason, the size or distance scales are set incorrectly, we should expect to find related perceptual distortions of size or distance. We should, therefore, enquire whether the distortion illusions are related to the particular kinds of sensory information used for setting perceptual size and distance of objects. This could be the key to the problem of illusions.

This is one approach to the problem, but there are quite different approaches. We might go directly to the actual components and circuits of the brain, while ignoring what may seem its basic processes. (This would be like looking at the 'hardware' of a computer while ignoring its 'programmes'.) It is often possible to repair a fault in electronic equipment by locating and replacing a burned-out component. This can be done with no understanding of the functional principles – or the programmes if a computer – of the equipment. But this is not quite the case we are considering. In the case of visual distortion illusions, we have a system which is functioning as expected except in these particular situations, when viewing certain shapes. Further, all examples of this system (all human observers) suffer much the same errors; and so the trouble certainly cannot be equivalent to a 'burned-out component'. A neurological abnormality may be due to the malfunctioning of components, but this cannot apply to this situation, because we are all similarly affected.

There is another possibility of circuit malfunction. Circuits may run into some kind of overload condition. This could occur with all observers in certain extreme situations. Indeed, we have already seen examples of this kind of thing in the after-effect of movement phenomena, and in after-images of brightness and of colour.

It is most probable that Op art provides examples of the overloading of, primarily retinal, visual circuits. The effects are not systematic distortions (or scale errors) but rather peculiar 'jazzing' effects, given particularly by rather closely spaced lines of extreme contrast.

Among the first artists to convey movement vividly was Van Gogh, with his wildly swirling brush strokes. But it is one thing to give an *appearance* of movement and quite another to so stimulate the eye that we *experience* movement. This is achieved by the Op artists, most successfully by Victor Vasarely (figure 76) and by Bridget Riley (figure 77). They abandon all hints of objects, and produce designs

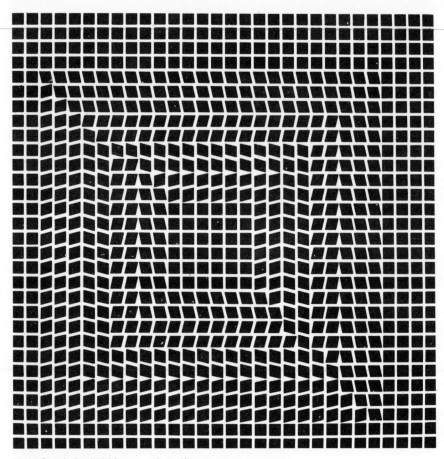

76. An Op painting (1964) by Victor Vasarely. This shifts and changes in curious ways. There is probably no single explanation. Eye movements contribute, but also we tend to 'organise' it in various ways, seeking objects in its pattern but never finding them. Abstract art may represent high-level abstractions of object-hypotheses.

which shift and float and shimmer, sometimes with violent though illusory movement. It is most likely that this sensation of movement is due to direct stimulation of the retinal movement detectors with the constant tremor of the eyes. At any rate, these effects seem to be due to pushing the neural systems beyond their normal functional limits and 'overloading' them. The effects are thus of the same general kind as those due to circuit faults, drugs or fatigue. This is not to say that such effects have no visual

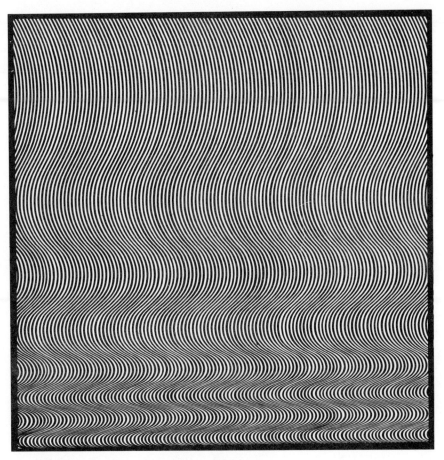

77. *Fall* by Bridget Riley. The powerful effects given by these Op paintings are largely mysterious. Eye movements play a part, by stimulating the on-off movement detectors of the retina and also by beating the repeated forms against displaced after-images, to give moiré patterns; but there may well be more to it. In any case, there is no reason why physiological explanations or lack of them – should reduce the visual interest of paintings.

interest: they can be exciting experiences in the hands of the artist who learns how to use such break-down effects to elicit experience. The kinds of movement which can be given by Op art techniques are limited, and it is difficult even though possible to endow recognisable objects with movement on a static canvas; but it may be true that the strong patterns which make their presence felt so dramatically with this curious shimmering and shifting may break up established routines, to help us see afresh.

79 *opposite*. As we should expect, distortion illusions occur not only in the skeleton perspective drawings of the 'illusion figures', but also in pictures and photographs of scenes having marked perspective features. This is an example.

Returning to our distortion illusions: is it likely that simple common shapes, such as the Muller-Lyer arrows, would 'overload' neural circuits? If so, it would reflect a remarkably poor design. But this seems unlikely. Although at this stage we cannot entirely reject the possibility, it seems implausible, given the remarkable efficiency of the visual system as a whole.

So let us take up the notion that the distortions may be due to mis-setting of size or distance scales. Perhaps the first hint of such an idea was given in 1896 by A. Thièry, who suggested that the distortion-illusion figures are essentially skeleton perspective drawings, suggesting depth. He thought of the Muller-Lyer arrows as drawings of objects such as a saw-horse, with the legs going into the distance for the outward-going arrows, or approaching with the inward-going arrows. Another, and better, example is any corner, such as in figure 68. The flat projection on the paper – and the image on the eye while looking at an actual corner – is the same shape as the Muller-Lyer illusion figure. Similarly, the Ponzo illusion gives the same projection as the receding lines, say, of a railway (figure 78).

78 *below*. The Ponzo distortion illusion. The upper bar of the parallel pair appears longer than the lower, though they are the same length. The distortion seems to be due to the convergence setting Constancy Scaling appropriately to the normal world of three-dimensional objects, when the upper part would be more distant, and so shrunk at the eye. Here, perspective is presented on the flat plane of the picture; and so the compensation, normally giving Size Constancy, is inappropriate. Instead of allowing us to see the two horizontal bars the same length, the one that would normally be shrunk by distance is seen in the picture as expanded. The fact that this scale change occurs though we do not see the figure in depth implies that Constancy Scaling can be set directly from typical depth-features at the eye, and not only by the prevailing hypothesis of depth as in the experiments with the reversing cube-objects. Evidently the stored perceptual hypotheses are scaled by typical depth-features, to fit the sizes and distances of external objects.

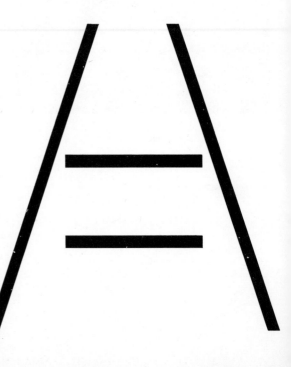

Now what is interesting is that the features indicated as *distant*, by a perspective interpretation in terms of the world of objects, are *expanded* in the illusion figures. We can see this clearly by comparing the skeleton illusion figures with photographs of typical scenes showing corresponding perspective. The line drawings and the photographs appear similarly distorted (figures 66–9).

Now if perspective depth information is used to set perceptual size or distance scales, we should not be surprised to discover that when perspective is given not – as normally – by the geometrical shrinking of retinal images with increased object distance, but by a figure *on a flat surface*, it sets the size scale inappropriately.

Objects normally appear very much the same size over a wide range of distances, in spite of the geometrical shrinking of their retinal images with object distance. There must, therefore, be perceptual compensation of size with distance. If perspective of the retinal image is a cue used to set this compensation, then we should surely expect that it would produce corresponding distortions when present at the eye without the different distances of objects which normally generate perspective shrinking with increasing distance. In other words, picture-perspective sets perceptual scaling inappropriately for a flat object – to generate distortion. Features indicated as distant should be expanded, which is the case.

It might be tempting to say at this point that the distortions are due to just the same effect as the size change with apparent-distance we saw with the reversing cubes, and with the Emmert's Law demonstration with after-images projected on to screens at various distances. But this will not do. In the illusion figures, distortion occurs *though the figures appear flat*. True they have marked perspective features, but we certainly do *not* have to *see* the Ponzo, the Muller-Lyer or the other figures as lying in depth for the distortions to occur. Though we see them lying flat on the paper the distortions still occur – but this is contrary to what we found with the reversing cubes. They only change shape when they are seen in depth: not when they are seen as flat drawings.

So we are presented with a problem. Are these distortions, after all, unrelated to perceptual size-distance scaling? Or are they related, but in some subtle way? The fact that the distortions go in the same direction as perceptual depth may suggest that there is a connection. But if so, what can this be?

Let us ask first: why are these, admittedly typical perspective drawings, not seen in depth? The answer to this seems clear. The depth indicated by these figures is *countermanded by the texture of the background*. This is

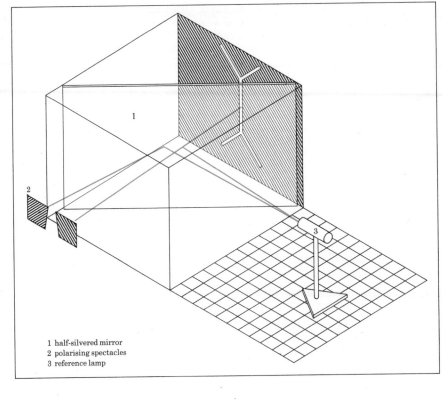

1 half-silvered mirror
2 polarising spectacles
3 reference lamp

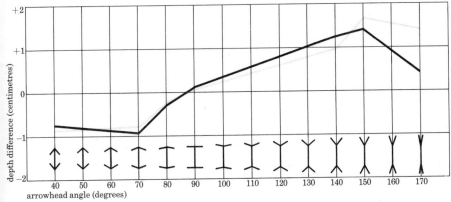

depth difference (centimetres)

arrowhead angle (degrees)

easily shown by removing the background and looking at them glowing in the dark by painting them with luminous paint. When the background is made invisible in this way the figures do generally appear in depth, according to their perspective features.

We can go further. We can objectively measure the apparent depth of the figures. We can then relate apparent depth to the extent of the distortion for any figure.

Measuring apparent depth in pictures

At first thought, one might think that it is strictly impossible to measure *apparent* depth. It seems so different from measuring the positions of objects in external space. How can we chart an observer's internal perceptual space?

It could be argued that we come close to it by simply getting someone (or indeed a trained animal) to touch objects at various distances. Or, perhaps better, to play a fairground game such as throwing rings on pegs placed at various distances. But although this would give some indication, errors would be difficult to interpret because they might be due to errors in the command signals to the limbs. It is indeed a deep problem how to distinguish between perception and performance behaviourally.

It is possible to devise a better way of measuring apparent depth. We can use the two eyes as a range-finder for measuring depth seen, by perspective or other depth cues, with a single eye.

First, it is essential to remove stereoscopic information, to measure the effect of perspective when presented on a flat plane. Secondly, we must remove the texture information of the background, to avoid the paradoxical contradictions of pictures. To remove stereoscopic information all we have to do is to present the figure to a single eye. To remove the background we make the figure luminous, so that its background is invisible. This can be done using photographic transparencies and back-illuminating with a rather dim even light. (An electroluminescent panel placed behind the transparency is ideal.) The problem now is to allow both eyes to see some kind of movable reference mark optically introduced into the figure.

The adjustable reference mark is a small disk of light – seen by both eyes – reflected from a part-reflecting mirror placed at 45° to the line of sight to the picture, which is viewed directly through the part-reflecting mirror. The reference light is seen in the picture because optically it *is* in the picture. If the optical path from the eyes to the light is greater than the distance of the picture, it will be optically behind the picture: if nearer, in front. Now it is only necessary to make the picture invisible to one eye while allowing both eyes to see the reference light. Then we can use the two eyes as a range-finder for indicating the apparent distance of any selected features of the picture for charting visual space. This we do by polarising the light from the picture, and cross-polarising at one eye. A sheet of 'polaroid' is placed over the transparency (oriented at 45° from the horizontal) and a second polaroid filter is placed over one of the observer's eyes, oriented at 90° from the first filter to cut out the light to that eye. Since the reference light is not polarised, *both* eyes see the light but only *one* eye sees the picture. Visual space is plotted by placing the light by the side of selected features, and moving it in or out until it is seen – by stereoscopic vision – as the same distance as that feature of the picture.

We do not have to use only one reference light. We can use several, each placed at the distance of selected features of the picture, to measure their apparent distances. We call this depth-measuring instrument *Pandora's Box* (figure 80).

What happens when we measure apparent depth in the illusion figures? Having removed the competing depth information (stereoscopic vision of two eyes and the background texture) we find that illusion figures, such as the Ponzo (railway line) and the Muller-Lyer (arrows) figures *do appear in depth, and are measured to appear in depth.* Further, by measuring the depth for figures having various perspective angles, we can relate apparent depth to distortion. An experimental result is given in the graph of figure 81. The result is that the distortions are very highly correlated with the depth, as measured in this way, for various angles of the perspective features of the figures.

It seems from these experiments that perspective can set visual scale directly – even when the perspective is countermanded by other information such as background texture so that depth is not seen. We know this because we still get the illusion distortions when the figures are on a textured background, of, for example, the pages of this book, and appear flat.

Now we come to a most important point. Going back to our reversible wire skeleton cube experiments, we found that they changed shape according to the apparent distance of the back and the front of the cube. When the cube reverses visually – though with no change at the retina – the apparent size of the back and front changes: the apparent back always appearing larger than the apparent front whichever actual faces these might be. But this effect must be different from the distortion of these perspective figures, for they are *distorted though no depth is seen.* We thus arrive at the conclusion that the distortions can occur in two different ways. They occur either because depth is *seen* or because depth is *indicated* by perspective but not seen because countermanded by background texture. There is no size distortion when the *indicated* depth and the *apparent* depth correspond to reality, but if either is incorrect there is a corresponding distortion of size.

We have seen that the distances of objects must be set by available sensory information, and evidently perspective of the retinal image is very important for this. When it is inappropriate to true distance it produces size errors. We have also seen that the shape of depth-reversing objects changes with each depth-reversal, though the retinal image remains unchanged. These are, then, two distinct ways in which size is scaled perceptually.

We may say that depth-reversal (of say the cubes) corresponds to selecting alternative object-hypotheses of what the image may be representing. But the hypotheses represent three-dimensional objects, which have typical sizes and shapes. So we arrive at the idea that size and shape can be scaled *directly from the object-hypotheses*. Selection of an inappropriate hypothesis – such as the reversed cube – selects inappropriate sizes for the front and back, and so it appears distorted though there is no misleading retinal information.

We may now compare what we believe is happening in perceptual distortions with what is, surely, the same problem in physics when instrumental readings are used to read reality, but with inappropriate scaling constants, as sometimes happens.

5 Scaling the universe

Just as machines are extensions of muscles, improving on their power and precision, so are scientific instruments extensions of the human senses. Instruments increase their range in time and space and allow measurement in terms of scales having agreed units. Some physical units are derived from dimensions of the body; a foot was the length of an adult foot, a yard a single stride. But although it is convenient to use physical standards so readily available as parts of our own bodies, we are not sufficiently standardised in size or in sensory capacity for such measures to have sufficient accuracy for more than the crudest crafts; certainly not for technology or science. The next step was to take a foot as the average of several adult human male feet – actually the feet of the first twelve men leaving church on a Sunday was commonly used in the Middle Ages. We know from the precision of some early buildings that accurate measurements were made with simple instruments several millennia BC, and intelligence was certainly applied to improve upon pure perceptual judgements of, for example, the horizontal. It is believed that the Egyptians achieved flat and level foundations for large buildings by first building a low wall and filling the enclosed area with a few inches of water to serve as reference. Much human intelligence has gone into augmenting our physiological limitations.

Early descriptions of the Universe are egocentric and based on the physical size and capacities of man. Instruments allowed other references to be used, and so subtly displaced individual perception from the centre of the human view of the world. They showed that there are many things in the Universe not only too small or too distant to perceive, but also things immediately present whose presence could not be felt; such as the great sweep of the electromagnetic spectrum from X-rays to radio waves, with only one octave – light – sensed and so known to the brain without instruments.

Although we can judge sizes and distances, even of distant objects, and this ability is vital to survival in a largely hostile world of objects, sensory systems are easily adapted and thrown out of calibration. We are, however, good at comparing lengths, or comparing intensities of light, and so using physical standards for measurement such as yardsticks, rulers or photometers. Used effectively, even simple instruments can improve sensory precision a thousandfold, though the sensitivity of eyes and ears approach the theoretical limits of any physically possible detectors.

When sensory information is used for guiding action, it must control movements which are appropriate to the positions and sizes of the surrounding objects. Sensory information must be scaled appropriately to the external world, for control and prediction to be possible. Similarly, the readings of instruments cannot be in arbitrary units but must, at least ultimately, be tied to familiar objects. Some measures are *direct* (such measures as length with rulers) while others are *indirect* (such measures as temperature with a thermometer).

All measures come down to adopting recognised procedures, including how to make the ruler the right length, or the standard candle or lamp the right intensity.

With the development of sophisticated indirect measurements, we see a technological parallel of the ancient development of the indirect senses of vision and hearing, probing out from the direct senses of touch and taste which directly monitored vital aspects of the immediate world. Vision demands that every received pattern be interpreted according to a theoretical construction of the world of external objects, and the same is true of all indirect measures in science. Both are used to suggest and test between alternative hypotheses. In both, the readings must be scaled; either according to procedures derived from the direct methods of measurement, or according to assumptions about the nature of the objects being measured.

We will develop this theme, that vision is logically like applying indirect measures in physics. Both require assumptions. Both depend upon direct measures. Both require scaling constants, derived from past success or failure to make the data fit the world. We will take an example of scientific measurement in some detail – measuring distances of stars.

Astronomers use both *direct* and *indirect* methods for measuring stellar distances. Direct methods are available for only a few of the nearest stars. For more distant stars special assumptions have to be made, and it is always possible that these assumptions are in error.

The distances of the nearest stars can be determined by a direct method which is equivalent to stereoscopic vision. It is geometrical, and like stereoscopic vision is essentially unambiguous, though it is a delicate matter and severely affected by small instrumental errors. The method uses the

82. Astronomers measure the distance of stars by their parallax shift across the curtain of very distant 'fixed' stars. The astronomer must know the length of the base (twice the distance of the sun) or all his measures will be systematically in error.

geometrical parallax shift of the nearer against more distant stars with a change of viewing position. Stereoscopic vision uses, of course, the differences of view given by the $2\frac{1}{2}$ in. separation between the eyes. Astronomers find that the diameter of the Earth is insufficient as a base-line for stellar objects. They do not use simultaneous observations, but take photographic plates at six-month intervals to use the diameter of the Earth's orbit – 186,000,000 miles – for the base. The first star whose distance was measured in this way was Barnard's star, by the German astronomer Bessel, in 1838. He obtained a parallax of 0·35". This has since been corrected to 0·3". This parallax corresponds to a distance of about ten light years. The largest known parallax of any star is less than 1" of arc, this being equivalent to an object 1 in. in diameter viewed from a distance of over 3 miles. The greatest distance which can be measured by this direct parallax method is about 300 light years (though we can see with the unaided eye the Andromeda Nebula some 2 million light years distant).

The light year is a unit which is not directly related to parallax measurements. There is, however, a directly related unit – the 'parsec'. (One parsec is the distance given by a parallax of 1", which is equivalent to a distance of 206,265 times the radius of the Earth's orbit: i.e. the distance of the sun, 93 million miles, which is an astronomical unit for distance. The term 'parsec' means *par*allax of one *sec*ond. In miles, one parsec is slightly less than 2×10^{13} miles, which is also 3·258 light years. The nearest star is 1·31 parsecs, or 4·2 light years distant from Earth.)

For comparison, stereoscopic vision has a useful range of a few hundred yards. Its range is so much smaller because the smallest angle the eyes can resolve is about one hundred times greater than the telescope, but, more important, the base-line – the difference between the eyes – is so very much less than the diameter of the Earth's orbit.

The greatest stellar distance that can be measured with this direct method is about 100 parsecs. Beyond this, a method equivalent to perspective is used. This is known as 'hypothetical parallax' and is based upon the observed fact that the sun (and so the Earth with it) is moving through space, with reference to a large number of stars, towards Vega, in the constellation Lyra. The motion of the sun generates apparent velocities to our neighbouring stars, and these velocities are a function of their distances – just as nearby landscape moves faster than distant objects seen from a moving car or train. Since it is possible to observe these stellar perspective shifts over a period of many years (now nearly a century of photographic records) distances much greater than those given by simple parallax from our orbit-base can be obtained. It is, however,

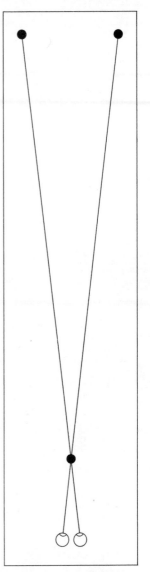

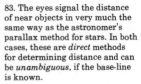

83. The eyes signal the distance of near objects in very much the same way as the astronomer's parallax method for stars. In both cases, these are *direct* methods for determining distance and can be *unambiguous*, if the base-line is known.

vital to separate shifts of the star positions due to movement of the observatory through space towards Vega, from the relative 'proper motions' of the individual stars. Our movement through space is itself statistically derived from observations of apparent motions of very many stars. The residual systematic movement is attributed to motion through the stars. It is a complex matter, requiring many observations and much calculation to derive this motion of the sun towards Vega; but it is precisely what the brain is called upon to do when we walk through a crowd, or drive in heavy traffic, or take part in formation flying. The limits of the brain's capacity for resolving velocity vectors given by dynamic perspective from many objects in relative motion is not known. It would make an interesting study.

Distances of more distant stars have to be measured with indirect methods, which are not geometrical. They all involve assumptions which cannot be directly tested.

Clearly, if all stars had the same intrinsic brightness then their relative distances could be obtained rather easily by accepting the inverse square law relating apparent brightness to distance. But absolute brightness (or 'magnitude') of stars is known to differ greatly, so apparent magnitude by itself gives no better than a very rough statistical guide to distances. It is, however, possible to classify stars, from their spectra and in other ways, into classes having known intrinsic brightness. It is then possible to use apparent intensity to estimate

84 *opposite*. This star field shows objects of very different brightness. On average, the apparently dimmest are more distant, but some of the faint objects are close, having low intrinsic brightness. They appear distant when in fact they are not. Apparent brightness is an *indirect* method for estimating distance: it involves assumptions about the external objects which may be wrong – leading to systematic errors.

85 *below*. Different spectral star types. The sun is an average kind of star, classified as an 'O' type. Other spectral types are associated with intrinsically dimmer or brighter stars. Having classified them, it is possible to estimate distance by applying a scaling constant. If this is inappropriate, systematic errors are made. These errors we regard as logically equivalent to visual distortion illusions.

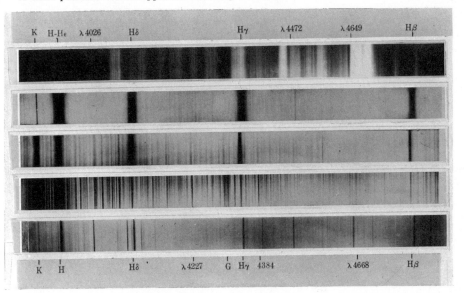

K H-Hε λ 4026 Hδ Hγ λ 4472 λ 4649 Hβ

K H Hδ λ 4227 G Hγ 4384 λ 4668 Hβ

distance: providing appropriate scaling constants are applied, both for the intrinsic brightness of the star itself and for any special factor producing loss of light between the star and the observer. Light might be partially lost by intervening gaseous cloud: this must be taken into account or there will be a corresponding error of the distance estimate judged from apparent brightness. A wrong scaling constant – and this is the point – will give errors equivalent to perceptual errors in mist or fog.

It is necessary to make assumptions about the object itself, about intervening conditions and about the measuring instruments and their calibrations before indirect methods can be applied, or systematic errors will be generated. Such errors seem to be equivalent to perceptual scaling errors, giving the visual distortion illusions.

Objects which are not classified for appropriate scaling constants cause great trouble. For example, it is not known whether the newly discovered stellar objects, quasars, are extraordinarily intense sources, and lying at correspondingly enormous distances, or whether they are in the normal range of brightness and so distance. The difficulty arises in their case because their spectra show a red shift of the lines, which would normally indicate a very high recession velocity, due to Doppler shift, itself believed to indicate great distance. So either there is some special reason for the red shift observed for quasars, or they are indeed very distant. But it is not yet agreed how the scaling constant should be set for quasars, and so it is not agreed whether quasars are incredibly bright and distant or whether they are nearer and of normal intensity, but have some peculiarity which upsets the generalised assumptions applied, apparently successfully, to other stellar objects for determining their distances.

It may seem a large jump, but the situation in astronomy over quasars is logically similar to the special problem that pictures present to the eye. Pictures present similarly doubtful scaling factors. Presenting perspective at the retina, but not due to geometrical shrinking with distance, the picture being actually flat, is just the kind of situation that would produce large errors in physical measurements, in situations where normally reliable assumptions do not hold. Freak conditions do upset indirect measures, but from this point of view pictures can be worse still – some are like the Piltdown Skull with false evidence planted deliberately to mislead the eye. Pictures are such artificial visual inputs that the surprising thing is not that they may appear ambiguous, uncertain, paradoxical or distorted representations of objects, but that we make anything of them at all.

Astronomical objects are also peculiar visual objects

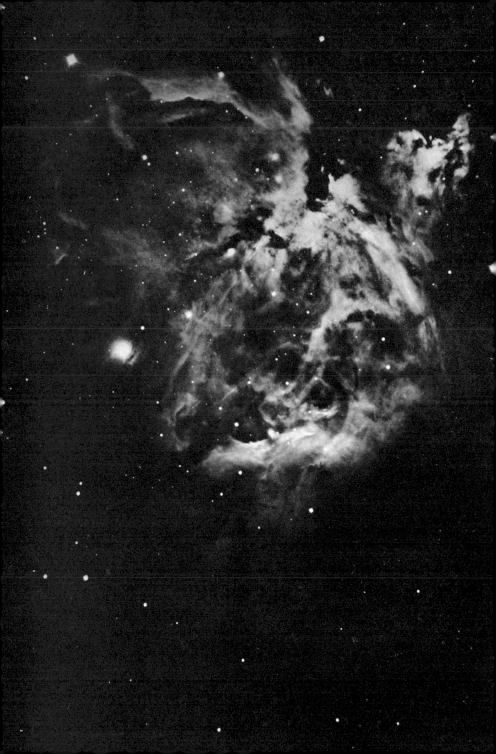

for which we cannot apply appropriate perceptual scaling
constants from direct experience.

How do we scale the moon and the stars?

The moon is perceptually interesting because, until
recently, it has not been touched. The moon provides a fair-
sized image (it subtends 0·5°, which gives an image of about
one-quarter the diameter of the foveal region of the retina).
Some detail is apparent to the unaided eye, and unlike the
sun it is of a comfortable brightness. The fact that we
cannot walk towards it and touch it, makes the moon a
heaven-sent object for perceptual study, while astronauts'
observation adds to the interest.

The distance and the size of the moon have been known
intellectually for at least the last 2000 years, since Hip-
parchus. Educated people know that it is about 240,000
miles away, that its diameter is about 2000 miles and that
it is a sphere. But this is not at all how it appears, even to
people fully aware of the physical facts about the moon as
an object. It appears as a disk, about a foot across and
perhaps one mile distant. It seems that we all see it as
having very much the same size and distance – so we all
see it with about the same error. It is the most enormous
mass illusion in history!

In fact the size and distance error is about a millionfold.
But it is not just the size of the illusion which is surprising,
but also that we attribute *any* size or distance to it. Vision
is essentially an *indirect* source of size and distance information: it is logically necessary that retinal images
should be calibrated against direct measures, such as
touching objects or walking towards them and recording
the size-change at the eye, but no such calibration is
possible for setting the scale of the moon. The fact that we
do attribute a size and distance is strong evidence for
supposing that the moon gives an object-hypothesis entirely based on other, familiar, terrestrial objects. Its perceived size and distance is probably set by a kind of
average of all objects giving its (rather small) retinal
image. At any rate, the fact that it is given a size and
distance shows that the perceptual system will take an
assumed scale in the absence of explicit scaling information, rather than infer that the object has *no* scale.

It is well known that the moon generally appears considerably larger when low on the horizon than when high
in the sky. We may say that the perspective, and other
depth-features of the ground visible before it, serve to
modify the 'null' scale of the moon.

Perhaps it is surprising that intellectual knowledge of
its physical scale does not affect how we see it. Although
perception is a kind of problem-solving activity, evidently

intellectual knowledge has little effect on perceptual solutions.

The fact that it appears larger near the horizon was discussed by Ptolemy. He suggested that when low it appears beyond the horizon, but that when high in the sky it appears nearer. He thus argued, in effect, that something like Emmert's Law applies to the moon. But it does not obey Emmert's Law; in fact it looks *nearer* on the horizon, when it looks larger. We may say that this is because our Primary Scaling is operating, to expand the moon though it looks no more distant, much as in the distortion-illusion figures. We should expect it to look nearer if it is, when perceptually expanded, equivalent to a larger luminous object suspended in a void.

To the Greeks, the stars were luminous points on a hollow sphere, with Earth as centre. This is still how we *see* the Universe though we *know* it to be quite otherwise. We see the sun as moving across the sky though we know that it is our rotation which is responsible.

When travelling, we see the moon and stars apparently following our every movement. Intellectually, we know that they are still but are so distant that there is no appreciable parallax change. For objects at terrestrial distances, absence of parallax change with our motion occurs only for objects moving with us – and so we see the heavens sharing our motions on Earth. Is it too fanciful to suppose that it is this which led man to believe that the stars do not merely look coldly down, but take an active interest in our individual affairs?

6

How concerned are artists with representing objects in the space of the three-dimensional world?

From the beginning art seems to have been associated with magic and religious, not merely physical, views of the world. Cave paintings seem to have had significance in terms of what we would call sympathetic magic. Perhaps pictures were regarded as talismans; as charms for good or evil capable of evoking thoughts and moods not only in men but also in the Gods: for they are found on cave walls almost inaccessible to human view. Sometimes they were painted in succession one upon another, as though the place of the paintings took on a magic quality. Something of this magic quality of art is associated with all religious paintings, including the Christian, and is with us still.

In our society pictures are valued in monetary terms far beyond 'reason'. An original painting may cost hundreds even thousands of times more than a virtually indistinguishable copy. A painting's value depends greatly on the artist and whether it is identified as genuine. It is something of a sacred object, even when its subject is profane. Evidently paintings are regarded as more than surrogate retinal images: they can be valued more highly than sight itself.

In religious paintings the subject was of first importance, for they were used for conveying and unifying belief among illiterate people. But what is portrayed is not always important. A bunch of grapes or a dead hare are not in themselves interesting or valuable, and yet a picture of such worthless objects can command more than a man earns in a lifetime. But is this conceivable if paintings are no more than representations of the shapes and colours of objects? It is indeed just because a painting is not simply a spatial record that it can have a value and an interest far greater than the objects it portrays.

It is striking how seldom accurate representation of space is found in art. Indeed many of the most prized paintings appear perfectly flat. Certainly the ability to represent depth is regarded as but one, and a minor, accomplishment, except in special cases. And yet paintings generally include objects which we normally see in depth. So there is a problem: why is depth so often neglected? In particular, why is strict geometrical perspective so seldom adopted? After all, the retinal image is in geometrical perspective (every feature halved in size with doubling of distance), so why does the artist seldom reproduce the eye's image to record depth in pictures? We may say at once that there is a very real difficulty in this. Although the retinal image is in strict perspective (like a

87. In Egyptian figure drawing the limbs take on strange contortions, as they have to fit the flat picture-plane without representation of depth. Also, the various parts of the body are shown in typical positions almost without reference to how they would lie in the particular pose. It is as though typical perceptual hypotheses are selected and combined without modification by scaling factors.

photograph) this is not how we see the world – because the image is effectively modified by perceptual scaling. Size scaling greatly reduces the perceptual shrinking of objects as represented optically at the eye: for this reason alone we should not expect artists to adopt strict perspective. But this can hardly be all there is to the matter, for at least to our eyes, used to perspective pictures such as photographs, geometrical perspective can convey depth very forcibly. Also, much art is totally lacking in perspective – when it certainly does not represent what the artist sees, after his retinal images have been scaled to give perceptual constancy. The Egyptians used no depth-cues at all. Their pictures are almost perfectly flat-looking. And yet we cannot believe that this is how the world appeared to the Egyptians: their statues, bronzes and wooden figurines are not flat but model the world as we see it.

It is possible that the Egyptians did not represent depth in their pictures because they followed a rigid long-lasting convention or taboo. But there is some internal evidence

107

against this, in pictures which certainly seem not to be decorative or ritualistic, but technical. What is interesting here is that the lack of depth prevents crucial features of the objects being seen; which must detract from the value of these pictures if indeed they have the technical use, for teaching and so on, they seem to have. For example there are several otherwise highly realistic drawings of crafts, such as furniture-making, in which every detail of the tools and how they are used is shown except *just where*

the tool is cutting (figures 88 and 92). To our eyes this is most odd, for much of the point of the picture is lost. It seems to imply that the Egyptians were simply not able to represent slanting surfaces, using even the most primitive perspective. If a picture is regarded as a special kind of object in its own right there may be no great virtue in depth being precisely represented – but its lack does demand an explanation in what are surely technical pictures.

The Greeks show slanting surfaces, and limbs are drawn foreshortened in their vase paintings, but probably they never employed strict geometrical perspective. It seems to be generally thought that objects were not depicted in realistic depth until as late as the early Italian Renaissance, after attempts by the artist-architect Giotto (1266–1337). Perspective was first developed successfully by Brunelleschi (1377–1446), who was an architect. In fact both contributed to Florence cathedral, Giotto designing the bell-tower and Brunelleschi the dome. It is tempting

88. Egyptian technical drawings. These show a craft, furniture-making, with details of the shapes of the tools and how they are used; but they do not show where the tools are cutting, because of the non-perspective, edge-on view of the surfaces of the furniture. This seems to indicate that the Egyptains were *unable* to represent sloping surfaces. (After H.S. Baker, 1966.)

to think that they and their fellow artist-architects developed and used perspective because it was useful for the technical problems of planning and designing important buildings involving new shapes. Perhaps it is worth describing something of what happened according to the records.

In the first half of the fourteenth century Giotto began to represent objects in space; though by the criterion of a geometrical perspective he did so imperfectly. Not until

89. Greek vase painting, showing foreshortening of limb but not true geometrical perspective. This is perhaps the nearest to perspective achieved in pictures before the Italian Renaissance.

Brunelleschi, early in the fifteenth century, was the problem finally solved (in panels, now lost, showing views of Florentine buildings), and in the *Gates of Paradise* (1425–52) in the Florence Baptistry, by Ghiberti. Ghiberti makes it clear that the scenes depicted, in low relief, in his doors were intended to be life-like. He says:

I strove in all measure to imitate nature as far as I could . . . they are all in frames so that the eye measures them and so true that standing at a distance they appear to be in the round. They are in very low relief, and in the plane the figures which are near appear larger and those which are far off smaller, as in real nature. And I have carried through the whole work with these measurements.

Alberti, also of this school, went so far as to make perspective peepshows so that the viewer would see the picture from the one position where the perspective is strictly correct at the eye, to give such a strong indication of depth that a perfect illusion of depth is created.

The principles of geometrical perspective were not set down formally until Leonardo da Vinci (1452–1519). None of his writing on perspective survives except for a few pages in the *Notebooks*. It was Alberti (cf. Gombrich, *Art and Illusion*, page 253) who first suggested that painting can be considered as a window through which we may look at the visible world. Leonardo developed this idea by suggesting that 'perspective is nothing else than seeing a place behind a pane of glass, quite transparent, on the surface of which the objects behind the glass are drawn'. This involves an essentially scientific concept: it is not given directly by vision.

Giotto was appointed master of the cathedral works in Florence in 1334, with the task of designing a magnificent bell-tower to harmonise with the existing cathedral building, which had been designed by Arnolfo di Cambio and started in 1295. It is clear that this cathedral was regarded as very important, not only by the Church but also by the townspeople, for three years after the building started Cambio was exempted from paying all taxes, under the following decree:

The Commune of the People of Florence, from the magnificent and visible beginning of the said work of the said Church, commenced by the same Master Arnolphus, hope to have a more beautiful and more honourable temple than any other which is in the region of Tuscany.

Evidently the project was of major importance to the people of Florence and so their good will would be important. When Giotto was made master of the cathedral works, he had to design his campanile to fit the cathedral and it had to look right from many view points. The relation of the tower to the cathedral was important, so spatially accurate drawings would be extremely useful. Perhaps it was this clear technical need which forced these artist-architects to develop techniques for perspective drawing.

It is interesting that Giotto designed his campanile (figure 90) to have 'negative perspective': it is considerably wider at the top than the bottom. This serves to counteract the usual appearance of tall buildings, that they are leaning backwards – because size scaling works imperfectly, especially when the viewer is looking upwards or downwards. It is often said that the Greeks used similar devices for their temples, and that this shows that they understood geometrical perspective. But perhaps the evidence is not as convincing as might at first be supposed. Consider the

Parthenon, on the Acropolis in Athens, built between
447 and 432 BC, under Pericles. It may appear to be
a simple rectangular building, but in fact it is not. The
corner columns are set closer together than the central
columns (6 ft separation at the corners and 8 ft at the
centre). The long horizontal (over 200 ft) of the peristyle
is curved upwards at the centre; while the corner columns
lean in slightly, as do the long walls. The columns themselves thicken slightly at their centre, to give the famous
entasis generally believed to prevent them from looking
'hollow'. The peristyle columns taper upwards. They are
6 ft 2 in. diameter at the bottom, but only 4 ft 10 in. at the
top. It is often said that these deviations from the rectangular were designed to compensate for optical illusions. But if so, should we not expect the deviations to go
the other way – except perhaps the *entasis* of the columns
– if the intention is to prevent the building seeming to
lean backwards?

It is generally believed that the Greek temple was developed from earlier wooden buildings, perhaps from the
pile houses of the early European lake-dwellers, the piles
becoming the columns and the cross-beams the horizontal
architrave. Wooden buildings are easily modified, so we
might suppose that they were modified by trial and error
until they looked right. They could have been copied in
stone, without the need of a formal theory of perspective.
But in any case, the deviations do not fit what we should
expect of a perspective system at least on any simple
interpretation. It is tragic that virtually no Greek painting
survives, but in the absence of clear evidence it seems most
probable that they did not have geometrical perspective.
Perhaps further study of Greek vase paintings with this
question in mind might decide whether perspective was
invented or reinvented in the Renaissance.

However this may be, and we would like to know the
answer, there does seem to be a sound reason for the
Renaissance interest in and active development of perspective for certain pictures. It was developed by men who
were painters and architects. They were concerned in
planning buildings and picturing their ideas for other
eyes, not only to produce a satisfying picture but to show
the nature of real or imagined objects *as they would appear
from various positions.*

Artists probably did not discover geometrical perspective simply by looking at scenes and drawing what they
saw directly. It is much more likely that perspective was
discovered through measurement, and was only applied
consistently with the aid of instruments, especially the
camera lucida and the *camera obscura*. These give optical
projections allowing the scene to be traced directly from

an image. It is known that the master of perspective, Canaletto (1697–1768), used a *camera obscura* for much of his work. He did not, however, allow himself to become a slave to its image, for as W.G.Constable says in his *Canaletto*:

In most of his paintings he was astonishingly close to the facts in detail. . . . Yet he would change the relative sizes and positions of buildings by such devices as rapidly vanishing perspective lines, or the adoption of two or more view points when painting an extensive view.

Although Canaletto had the knowledge and the technical means for obtaining precise geometrical perspective, he seldom and probably never used it without modification to suit his artistic needs.

Photography does give pictures which are in strict geometrical perspective. The results can be most disappointing. Distant mountains lose their power to impress because they appear far too small. We have to some degree learned to accept the true perspective of photographs, but even so the expert photographer is forced to use telephoto lenses for distant objects – to simulate as nearly as possible perceptual size scaling – and even then he is not always successful in making his picture dramatic or 'real'.

If we are right in thinking that strict perspective is seldom used because precise spatial relations are generally unimportant to the artist, we should ask: what is important about pictures? Here we might gain a clue from the art which is most free of depth – Egyptian art.

91. The Egyptian God of the Nile. He is shown as a hermaphrodite, with both breasts on the same side. As in children's drawings, features may be misplaced in curious ways, each feature being shown from a typical view.

Pictures in Egyptian art are essentially like 'Identikit' pictures. They are combinations of 'standard views' of parts of the body and facial features. The standard view of each feature is characteristic and typical. Eyes are shown from the front, though the face is in profile; the shoulders and trunk are usually shown from the front though the rest of the body is in profile. This gives a queer disconnected effect. It can force the artist into redesigning the human

92. Another example of Egyptian drawing in which, apparently, the artist was unable to represent sloping surfaces, so losing vital depth information.

body, as in the placing of both breasts on the same side in the hermaphrodite God of the Nile (figure 91) or the strange malformation in figure 87.

The nineteenth-century engineer James Nasmyth was struck by the pyramid-like appearance of the sun's rays as converged by perspective. In his autobiography he wrote:

On many occasions, while beholding the sublime effects of the Sun's Rays streaming down on the Earth through openings in clouds near the horizon, I have been forcibly impressed with the analogy they appear to suggest as to the form of the Pyramid, while the single vertical ray suggests that of an Obelisk. . . . In the Louvre . . . I found a small pyramid, on the upper part of which appeared the disk of the Sun, with pyramidal rays descending from it to figures in the Egyptian attitude of adoration. This consists of the hands held up to the eyes – an attitude associated with the brightness of the Sun, and it still survives as the Salaam. *It also survives in the disk of the Sun, which has for ages been placed like a halo behind the heads of sacred and exalted personages, as may be seen in Eastern and early paintings, as well as in church windows at the present day.*

Nasmyth, who was a competent artist and son of a well-known Scottish landscape painter, illustrated the pyramid

93 *below left*. An Egyptian house-
hold pyramid, showing the sun's
rays and the uplifting of the
hands, perhaps originally to
protect the eyes from the sun and
later a gesture of respect or
reverence. (Etching by James
Nasmyth.)

94 *below right*. The form of the
pyramid may have been suggested
by the perspective convergence
of the sun's rays. It seems just
possible that if the Egyptians had
understood perspective they
would not have bothered to build
the pyramids. (Etching by James
Nasmyth.)

idea with an etching (figure 94). His example from a small
pyramid in the Louvre is shown in figure 93. Is it possible
that had the Egyptians understood perspective – and its
geometrical origin – they would not have built the
pyramids?

It is not just that perspective is not used in Egyptian art:
there is no consistent view of the objects as a whole. The
pictures are combinations of typical views of individual

features or parts of objects – orientation and position in
space is entirely secondary. They are sacrificed to represent the crucial features in typical orientations.

We find this same emphasis on typical views in the
Egyptian pictographs. Birds are shown in side view; eyes
from the front, and so on. Is it possible that familiarity
with the standard pictograms inhibited the Egyptian artists from giving consistent views by appropriately orient-
ing the parts of objects and figures?

It is a truism to say that artists represent their own
private view of the world. We may consider the notion of
'object-hypotheses' in this context. It is reasonable to
suppose that it is largely his object-hypotheses which
the artist represents. And they are units of his private
world. Now, we have argued that the object-hypotheses
cannot contain information of scale, distance or orientation – because objects can be in any position in space relative to the observer. This implies that they must normally
be scaled to fit the prevailing situation, by current sensory
data. So we may suppose that they represent *typical* views
and sizes, these being modified by available sensory infor-

95. Drawing by a child aged six.
Child art is remarkably similar to
Egyptian drawing, in showing
queer combinations of typical
views of parts of the body.

mation during perception. If what the artist represents is
largely what is stored in his brain – his 'object-hypotheses'
– then we should expect that his pictures will lack the
scaling normally imposed on object-hypotheses to make

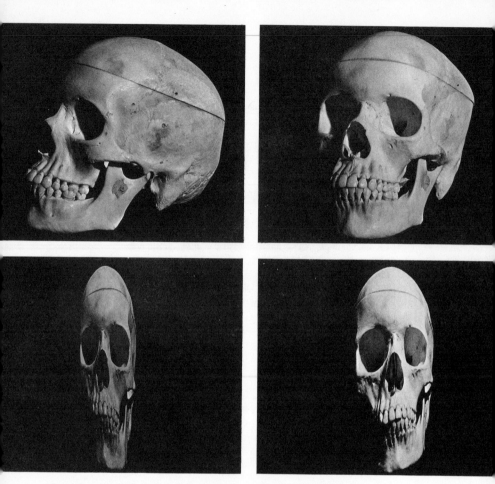

them fit a particular situation. From the evidence of child art, it seems to be remarkably easy for human beings to draw typical views of common objects, but difficult to draw *atypical* views, with the perspective associated with a *particular* viewing position. In this sense, Egyptian and child art are similar. Indeed, it is interesting how long it takes an art student in our culture to draw a lifelike figure, and it seems that a knowledge of anatomy helps. He has to develop his object-hypotheses. The artist needs rich object-hypotheses before he can perform spatial transformations to represent particular views.

Our experiments with the simple rotating wire figures casting shadow projections on a screen are relevant here. They show how all but the simplest and most familiar objects are not represented by object-hypotheses allowing

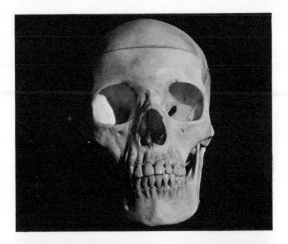

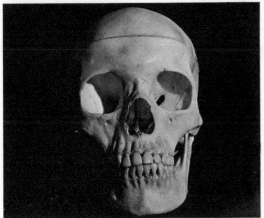

96–8. Views of an object as it is rotated. The retinal image undergoes the same transformations for an object rotated that we see in these photographs.

99–101. Views of a *picture* of the same object viewed as it is rotated. The retinal image undergoes the same transformations for a picture from various positions.

prediction of projections at the retina with each new orientation of the object. Taking now a familiar solid object, rather than the skeleton figures used for those experiments, we may look at the kind of transformations which occur with changes in orientation (figures 96–8). For comparison, we may also look at the transformations of the plane projection – a picture – of this object with changing orientation (figures 99–101). The brain, and the artist, have a difficult problem!

It should not, then, be surprising that artists give a personal view of the world – that they 'show through' their work – for they present combinations of their object-hypotheses. Only special training gives 'objectivity'. Pictures make us see things differently, by changing our object-hypotheses. This is the power of art.

102. An ordinary teacup?

117

103. Meret Oppenheim *Lunch in Fur*, 1938. A shocking combination which deeply affects us.

104. A visual pun, by Man Ray. It is surely our knowledge of the *non*-optical properties of irons and spikes which gives this its effect.

In modern art, games with object-hypotheses as 'counters' are most explicitly played by the Surrealists. Salvador Dali, René Magritte, Meret Oppenheim are surely affecting us by placing their object-hypotheses in punning combinations, which can be shocking or funny. For an example we may take Oppenheim's *Lunch in Fur* (figure 103). It is impossible to look at this picture without squirming! It is an outrageous pun – and so it is remarkably evocative.

If it is true that artists rely heavily upon their object-hypotheses, what happens when they try to draw totally unfamiliar objects? This might be the subject of an interesting experiment, but we have some data from the history of science, where careful observers have tried to describe and to draw objects never before available in detail to the human eye. There are many examples, from the early microscopists and the first users of telescopes who turned their instruments to the moon and planets.

The first telescopic observations were made by Galileo, between 1609 and 1619, using a primitive refractor of 1 in. aperture. Galileo was most puzzled by the appearance of the planet Saturn. We are of course very familiar with the fact that it has a ring, clearly seen in a small telescope. But Galileo had no idea of such a thing, and for a long time failed to see it correctly. He reported it as a triple object. When he did realise it was a ring he failed to report it at the time.

The Dutch scientist Christiaan Huygens built his own telescopes, and probably they were superior to Galileo's, but he also failed to see Saturn's ring correctly. Figure 106 shows a series of illustrations he drew with what is in fact the ring at various angles. Almost all are impossible. We must, however, be careful here, for fluctuation of the telescope image by atmospheric disturbance may produce fleeting distortions; but even so the errors in drawings (1), (4), (10), (11) and (13) could hardly be produced, and would not be drawn by anyone knowing the 'answer'. Huygens did finally manage to establish that the planet is surrounded by a 'thin, flat ring, nowhere attached to the body of the planet'. It is in fact difficult to see with small instruments and it is only visible at fleeting moments of best 'seeing' with the largest. Drawings do not represent how the object appears through a telescope at any one time. They are a synthesis of very many observations. They represent belief in what it is 'really' like. Indeed, it may be doubted if it is possible to make a single 'observation' of anything – for observation is in terms of object-hypotheses and they take time and knowledge to develop.

It is tempting to regard artists' pictures as representing not so much the world as they see it at any one time, but

105. The surprise shows us the (false) assumption we have accepted!

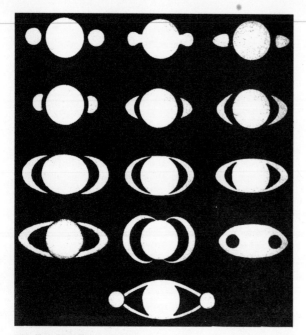

106. Christiaan Huygens' drawings of the planet Saturn. He did not know that it is encircled by a ring. Without the appropriate 'object-hypothesis' of the ring, he could not draw – or see – it correctly.

rather compositions of stored object-hypotheses. The object-hypotheses cannot contain distance information of objects, which may lie at any distance from the observer, so they have to be scaled for distance and orientation by currently available sensory information. So if paintings represent primarily what is stored in the brain of the artist – following what we believe is vital for all perception – then it is not too surprising if representation of distance and orientation came late in the history of art and were developed for technical purposes, when pictures were used as tools rather than works in their own right.

Neither pictures nor language work well for unique cases, for there must be shared perceptual hypotheses for communication to occur. If indeed pictures are a kind of language, painting is more poetry than prose.

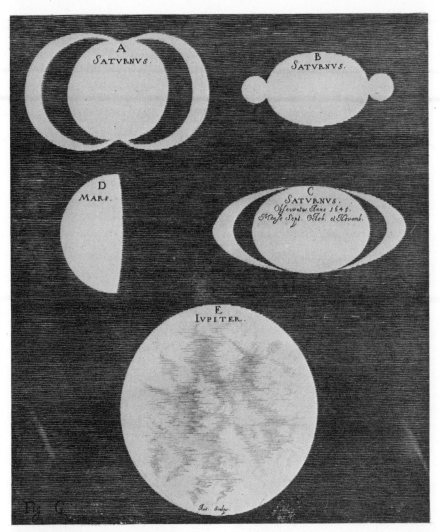

107. Early drawings of Saturn and other planets by Hevelius. He, also, appears to have interpreted his retinal images with an inappropriate perceptual hypothesis of the nature of Saturn's ring.

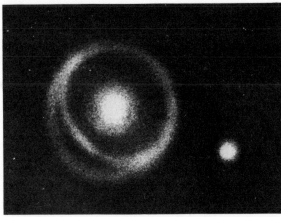

108 *opposite*. A series of photographic views of Saturn's ring, as it presents different aspects to Earth. For us, it is easy to interpret these photographs, but would it be so if we did not already know that it is a globe with a thin encircling ring?

109 *left*. Herschel's drawing of the nebula M 51, in the mid-nineteenth century. We now know it to be spiral.

110. Drawing by Ross of the same nebula, M 51. He knew it to be spiral in form.

111. Modern photograph of the same spiral nebula, M 51, taken with the Mount Wilson 100 in. telescope. There is perhaps sufficient visual information available to select an appropriate perceptual hypothesis, given no special prior information. Hence the importance of adequate and, so far as possible non-ambiguous, data for seeing, and for suggesting and testing, hypotheses in science. This is especially important when the truth happens to be unlikely on currently available data – as was the case with spiral nebulae at the time of Herschel.

We will now try to put to use some of the things we have learned about the perception of objects represented in pictures. Essentially, we have found that pictures – perspective or zero-perspective projections of objects – are remarkably unsatisfactory for representing clearly and unambiguously the three-dimensional structure of objects. This will come as no surprise to artists, who have been all too well aware of the difficulties and the short-comings of pictures for a very long time. Leonardo da Vinci wrote: 'If nature is seen with two eyes, it will be impossible to imitate it upon a picture so as to appear with the same relief, though the lines, the lights, shades and colour be perfectly imitated.' He did not however realise that the two views of the eyes (giving the so-called 'disparity' of the retinal images) are fused by the brain to give stereoscopic depth. The first hint of this is surprisingly late – Joseph Harris's *Treatise on Opticks*, of 1775. Harris comes to realise that the different view of the eyes can be combined by the brain, for he says:

And by the parallax on account of the distance betwixt our eyes, we can distinguish besides the front, part of the two sides of a near object . . . and this gives a visible relievo to such objects, which helps greatly to raise or detach them from the plane, on which they lie: Thus, the nose on the face, is the more remarkably raised by our seeing each side of it at once!

Evidently Harris does not mean the picture plane, for at that time the stereoscope had not been invented. No one had yet seen stereoscopic pictures.

The stereoscope was invented by the English physicist Charles Wheatstone, probably in 1833, though he did not describe it until 1838. It was a beautifully simple idea: to place a pair of pictures, one before each eye, the pictures representing the view points of a pair of eyes. What Wheatstone found was truly surprising. He found that pure line drawings, with no shading or any other hint of depth, were seen in distinct and clear relief. The lines of the drawing stood out clear from their background, as though entirely separate from it. In our terms, he totally removed the picture-plane paradox at one stroke, by entirely separating the picture from its background.

Several types of stereoscope were designed in the mid-nineteenth century. But one might ask: why is any instrument necessary? Why cannot we simply place a pair of suitable pictures one before each eye? The reason is two-fold: first, most people find it very difficult to keep the axes of the eyes aimed horizontally when looking at near objects; there is a strong tendency to converge the eyes to the 'point of fixation'. Secondly, the pictures would have to be very small; for it is difficult to accommodate nearer than about 10 in. from the eyes, and since the eyes are only separated by $2\frac{1}{2}$ in., they must be small or they would overlap when the eyes are aimed parallel at them. Some people can, however, over-converge and view a pair of pictures with crossed vision (figure 112). (In this way it is possible to dispense with any instrument, but it is tiring and not very satisfactory.)

Wheatstone used a pair of mirrors, one before each eye, oriented at 45° to allow pictures placed at either side to be fused by the eyes (figure 113). David Brewster invented an alternative system, using lenses, in 1849. Here the pictures are small but enlarged by the lenses, which combine

112. Stereo vision given by crossing the eyes, with a pin. The right eye sees the left picture and vice-versa. This enables rather larger pictures to be fused than is possible with normal vision without optical aid. It is not however very satisfactory.

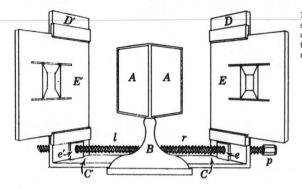

113. Wheatstone mirror stereo-scope. The stereo pair of pictures can be large, the mirrors allowing the eyes to converge in a normal manner.

deviating prisms so that the centres of the pictures can be further apart than the separation of the eyes and yet be fused (figure 114). This instrument is more compact than Wheatstone's mirror arrangement, and well suited to photographs having sufficient definition to stand enlargement by the viewing lenses. It came into use in Victorian drawing-rooms by the early 1850s when daguerrotypes and calotypes also came into general use. Indeed, stereo-scopy dates almost from the beginning of photography, but lost its popularity at the end of the century, except for scientific work. It is due for revival.

Stereoscopic cameras are available. They are essentially Siamese twins, two lenses in one body with a single roll of 35 mm. film. Each lens gives a picture from the view point that one eye would have. The pictures can be viewed either in a hand viewer, based on Brewster's stereoscope (though the pictures are so small that normal lenses, without prisms, are all that is required) or by projection. With this method the transparencies are projected super-imposed on a silver screen from a pair of slide projectors. Light from each projector is polarised at 45° from horizontal, and 90° from each other. The viewer wears special glasses containing polarising filters, oriented so that the light from the projector giving the right eye's view enters only the right eye and the left eye views only the left picture. The effect can be extremely realistic, especially with colour film, except that movements of the head do not produce motion parallax. Movements of the head make the stereo picture appear to rotate *with* the observer, as though the near features were somehow attached to his head.

It was soon discovered that if the right-eye picture is switched with the left-eye picture, depth is usually – though not always – reversed. The exceptions are most interesting. It is impossible, for example, to see a face

114 *opposite*. Brewster's lenticular prism stereoscope. This uses smaller pictures, which are magnified. The magnifying lenses are also prisms, allowing the centres of the pictures to be further apart than the separation of the eyes. With modern high-resolution 35 mm. transparencies this is not necessary: the modern equivalent uses still smaller pictures, more magnification with no prismatic deviation. (From the author's collection.)

115 *opposite*. Picture of the *inside* of a face. This is a photograph of a hollow mask – but does it look hollow? It is impossible not to see it as a normal face. Here the improbability of this being a hollow and not a normal face is so great that the truth is totally rejected.

116 *overleaf left*. Stereo picture of a normal face. What happens if the glasses are reversed, to give reversed stereo vision? Does the face look inside out or normal?

117 *overleaf right*. Stereo picture of a hollow mask. Does stereo vision make this look – as it is – hollow? Is stereo information sufficient to overcome the prior improbability of this being an inside-out face?

hollow, with the nose sticking in and not out of the face (figures 115–17). A statue in a hollow niche will appear, with pseudoscopic vision (as it is called) quite normal, but the niche will be depth-reversed so that the statue will stick out from the wall, not in. (The reader can try switching his eyes to give pseudoscopic vision, with the stereo pictures in this book, by holding the handle of the glasses with the left hand.)

This rejection of stereoscopic information giving an extremely unlikely answer to the ever-present perceptual problem – what and where is this object, if it is an object? – is a striking example of the intelligence of the Intelligent Eye.

There is nothing impossible about noses sticking inwards. If we look at the back of a mask, close-to in a good light, we see it as a hollow face. There is sufficient depth-information to overcome the improbability of a face being hollow. But when the mask is viewed in a poor light, or an even light casting no shadow or texture, it generally appears as a normal face, though in fact it is inside out. It takes the full power of stereoscopic and texture depth-information from the eyes to convince the visual brain to reject its usual perceptual hypothesis – which as we know from cartoons requires so little information to evoke for a face – that it is a face with the nose sticking out. When the inside of a mask appears as a normal face, it will swing round to follow the moving observer, in the same odd way that projected stereoscopic pictures move with the observer. In the case of the hollow mask – or reversed wire cube – this movement is twice as great, for there is motion parallax (because there are physically different distances), but the changing parallax is interpreted as due to a rotation in the opposite direction to the true sense when back and front are visually reversed. It is well worth looking at this effect with a hollow mask and with a wire cube. The effect may have been the basis of ancient temple miracles: statues moving as though alive, following each devotee with their hollow heads as he moves in the gloom of the sacred place.

The first stereograms made by Wheatstone were simple geometrical drawings, showing cubes, cylinders and so on in stereoscopic depth. The drawings were made using projective geometry, to reproduce the views of the two eyes. This technique has been used occasionally since.

It occurred to the author a few years ago that a simple device for drawing stereo pairs automatically might be interesting and useful. The first device that we made for drawing in 3-D is essentially optical, drawings being made by moving a point of light in three-dimensional space.

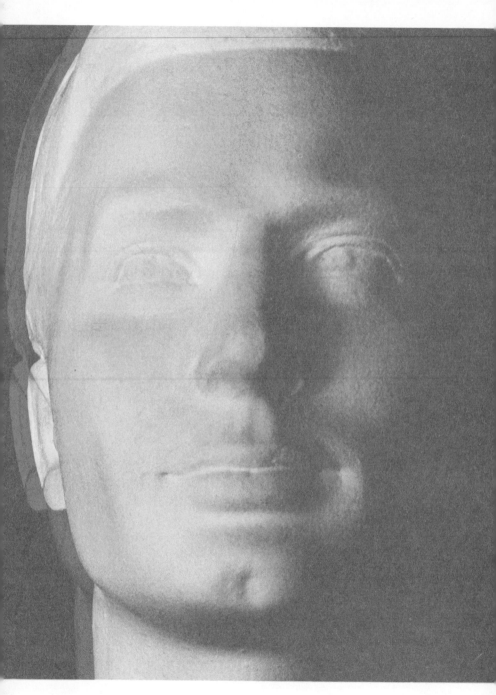

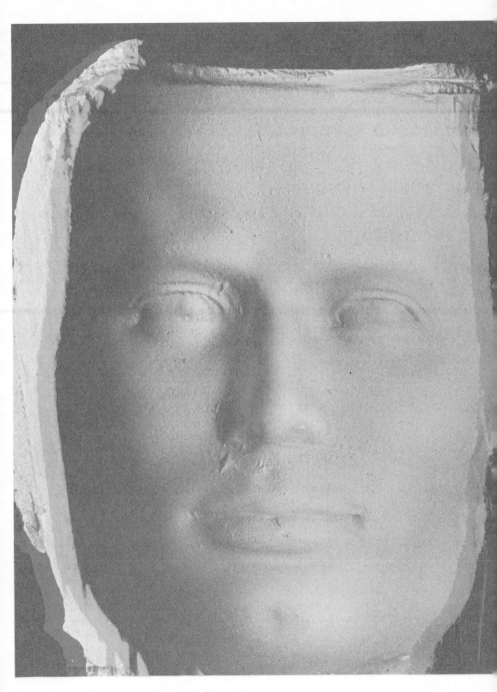

Suppose one had a stereo camera and a small light-source, it would clearly be possible to draw in 3-D by holding the shutters of the camera open in a dark room and moving the light-source about in front of it. By tracing the real or imaginary outlines of objects in three dimensions with the light, a stereo pair would be built up in the camera, for it would 'see' the source from its two points of view. This would hardly be a practical method though, because we could not see the stereo drawing until it was completed and the film developed. It would thus be like drawing with one's eyes shut, but more difficult because the hand movements are in three dimensions (figure 118).

To pursue this idea and make it practical, we must find some way of making the optically produced lines visible immediately and continuously while the drawing light is in motion. This can be done by using a phosphor in place of the film in the camera. By placing plates coated in phosphor in a suitable stereoscope, and also arranging for a pair of camera lenses to image the drawing light on the phosphor plates, we produce a pair of trails of light on the plates which are stereo pairs of the moving light. By looking into the stereoscope and moving the light it is possible to draw in three dimensions, the lines being luminous against a dark background.

This arrangement is strictly limited in its use, because phosphors lose their brilliance too rapidly. So we must use something which will remain glowing for a much longer time than a phosphor. This has recently been made possible by the development of electroluminescent image-retaining panels, which glow by electroluminescence after stimulation by light. The resulting picture is erased by switching off the (100 v. DC) power supply to the panels.

Figure 120 shows a practical arrangement for making a 3-D drawing machine using these panels for storing the pictures. It is quite fascinating to use.

There are quite other possibilities for 3-D drawing. We have already seen that it is possible to project in stereo depth three-dimensional objects, simply by casting a pair of shadows from horizontally separated point-sources on to a suitable screen and separating the shadow projections to the two eyes, with colour filters or with polaroid. We can make stereo drawings from these shadow projections, simply by tracing them with suitable coloured ink pens, and viewing through corresponding two-colour spectacles. This is a useful method for obtaining stereo drawings of existing objects, provided they are suitable for shadow projections. They should be essentially skeleton structures, made of wire, but can have any degree of complexity provided important features are not hidden, or masked, by other features.

A most interesting application for shadow-projected stereo is the showing of anatomical or crystal models. They may be projected to fill a large screen for viewing by an audience, and as the model can be rotated it can be shown from any position while the resulting motion parallax during rotation adds to the stereo information for giving unambiguous depth-information for strange shapes, where it is most important. Using two-colour separation (though not polarisation) it is possible to use semi-transparent plastic anatomical models for stereo projection. The result is most effective: internal structures can be seen in their correct positions through the structures within which they lie.

It is possible to draw directly on to paper (or better, back-illuminated opal glass) with quite a simple mechanical device. This is essentially a pair of differently coloured pens (red and green) held in a device which keeps them horizontally separated though free to move over the drawing surface, with an easily operated adjustment for changing their separation to give corresponding changes in visual depth. The further apart the pens, the nearer the stereoscopically fused lines appear to lie. The mechanical system for keeping the pens horizontal, and for changing their separation, is shown in figure 119.

This simple arrangement can be combined with the stereo-shadow projector. If the drawing surface is a sheet of opal glass (this is better than ground-glass, for it is less directional, but ground-glass must be used with polaroid filters) then it can be illuminated from the back not just by a single light, but by the pair of point-sources used for the stereo shadow projection. A model can be placed behind the screen and traced in depth. A reference grid on adjustable rulers can be projected in this way, as aids for drawing in depth.

It is also possible to combine a 3-D drawing machine with stereo-projected photographs. These can be projected on the drawing surface and can be traced or modified with the pair of differently coloured pens. In fact, a whole range of possibilities are opened up which might be useful to designers, and to engineering and medical students who often find considerable difficulty in conceiving and thinking precisely about three-dimensional structures.

There is a particularly attractive feature about doodling and sketching designs in 3-D. In normal drawing it is necessary at least to indicate surrounding structure in order to specify the position and scale of a feature. For example, an architect in a preliminary sketch, may find it hard to indicate the position in the third dimension of, say, a window without drawing something of its wall, and

118 *overleaf top*. Towards a 3-D drawing machine. Stereo camera with a moving light-source. This will give a stereo pair of the movements, in three dimensions, of the light. If one could see the 3-D picture as it was produced, this could form the basis for a practical 3-D drawing machine.

119 *overleaf bottom*. A simple mechanical '3-D blackboard', designed by the author. A pair of red and green pens are carried horizontally to any part of the drawing surface. Depth is given by adjusting the separation of the pens with the knob control which is geared to separate the pens as it is rotated.

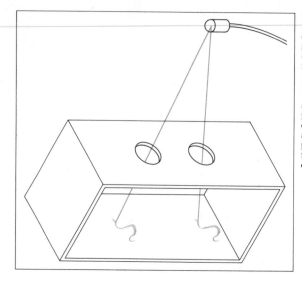

120 *opposite*. A practical design for a machine for drawing in 3-D, designed by the author. Photographic plates are replaced by electroluminescent image-retaining panels. These continue to glow after stimulation by light, so the moving pair of spots from the imaged point-source give an immediately visible stereo pair of all movements of the drawing light. The large mirrors and the reversing telescopic eye-pieces give correct visual depth for every direction of movement of the drawing light.

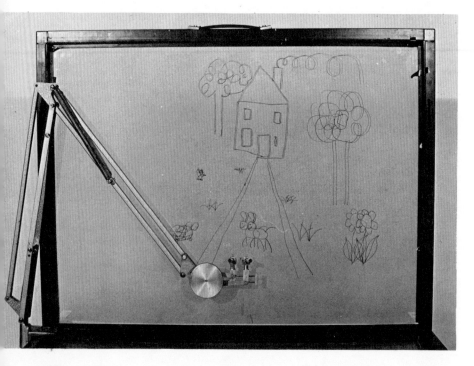

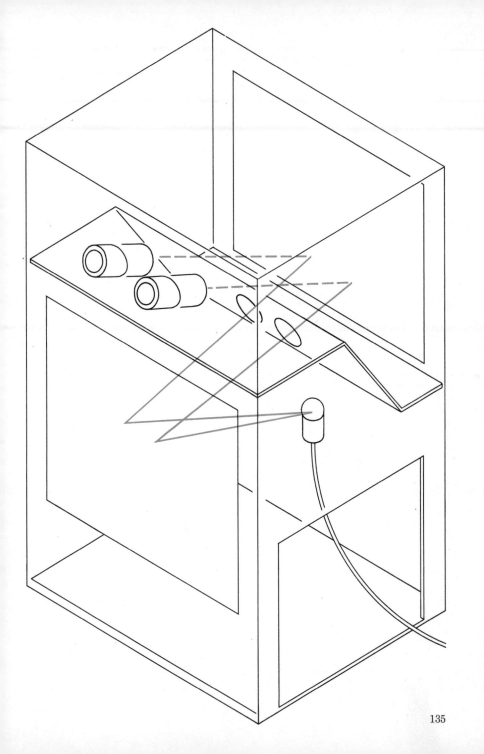

where its wall lies with respect to other features of the building. But suppose he has not yet considered the wall, only that he wants a window in a certain place. This is difficult to represent, but with 3-D drawing he can put his window where he wants it and then consider its surrounding features. In other words, 3-D drawing machines could be useful thinking tools for designing structures, and for communicating initial ideas and fully-worked-out designs.

It would be very interesting to try to improve the pre-precision of people's – perhaps especially children's – perception, using 3-D drawing machines. Perhaps by using them as tools, allowing active movement and related perception in three dimensions, our object-hypotheses could be developed to greater precision for seeing and designing the queer structures used by our society.

8 Pictures, symbols, thought and language

The fact that we can see pictures both as objects in their own right and as other objects 'shown' in them is remarkable enough. Even more remarkable is our ability to use certain shapes as *symbols*, to aid our own thought and to communicate with other people distant in space and time.

A great deal is known of the history of writing. The early symbols are preserved in many ways: on the rock walls of caves, on ivory, bone and metal, on the papyrus reeds used by the Egyptians and the skins used by the Semitic people responsible for the Dead Sea Scrolls.

It is interesting that the earliest drawings are never fully representational, but are cartoon-like pictures of familiar things, often hunting scenes (figure 121). It is not known whether the cartoon-pictures which survive developed from earlier more representational pictures, or whether the first pictures were cartoons, in which men and birds and beasts are shown with just a few lines. Early Chinese ideograms are remarkably similar to Egyptian hieroglyphics though separately invented. A feature of all ideograms is that the signs do not have to picture the whole of an object. One might say that they are cartoons of cartoons.

The ideographic scripts became, gradually, systems of writing related to the spoken words in use at the time. This occurred first with the Mesopotamian, Egyptian, Cretan and Hittite scripts, which all developed sound-associations. Written languages which can be spoken are of two kinds. Words may be represented by written characters representing spoken *syllables*, or they may be the symbols of an alphabet. Neither the symbols used in alphabets nor the symbols used in syllabic languages (ancient cuneiform and hieroglyphics, as well as modern Japanese and Chinese) entirely lose their picture quality.

The first full language was developed in the fourth millennium BC by the Sumerians. This is the cuneiform (Lat. *cuneus* 'wedge' and *forma* 'shape') script. It is found, impressed on clay tablets, in Mesopotamia, and was deciphered in the nineteenth century. The earliest writing found in this region was not cuneiform, but a

121. A cave painting. The figures are shown in dramatic movement, and are very effective cartoons. Representational drawing came after cartoon drawing – or is lost. Most likely it developed after cartoons in which perceptually essential features are selected.

picture-writing employing some 900 different symbols. This gradually became simpler, until the original picture symbols can only just be distinguished. (Curiously, the symbols were rotated from their original orientation, at about 3200 BC, for the symbols on clay tablets. On stone, they were rotated some centuries later.) It is these ancient, rotated pictograms which became the cuneiform characters of the first written language.

At this stage an important addition was made to simple picture writing. As the characters were used to express not only specific objects but also abstract ideas, one symbol took on many different meanings – and so the symbols became ambiguous. The problem was solved by adding *determinatives*. These were not spoken, but were used to indicate to the reader which of many meanings a symbol was intended to have. The determinatives were not specially invented, but were drawn from existing ideograms. Other determinatives were used to indicate how a given character should be spoken – much as we use an 'e' at the end of a word to determine the pronunciation of an earlier syllable, for example, 'fin(e)'.

Better known than cuneiform is the ancient Egyptian hieroglyphic writing. The word comes from the Greek *hieros* (holy) and *glyphein* (to carve), though it was

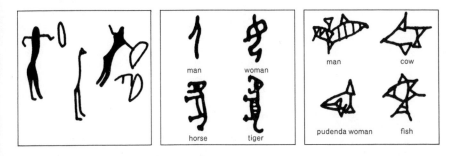

man   woman

horse   tiger

man   cow

pudenda woman   fish

used also for non-religious writing. The Egyptians themselves called it *mdw-ntr*, meaning 'speech of the Gods'; *mdw-ntr* may seem a little hard to pronounce. They did not use special symbols for vowel sounds, except sometimes for the beginning of a word, though they did, of course, have vowel sounds in their spoken language. Vowels were sometimes added in texts perhaps used for teaching, such as medical texts. Actually it is possible to read English without vowels. 'Th Gptns wr vr clvr' can be read. Context helps, though of course mistakes are quite frequent. Written vowels are particularly useful for reading aloud, but it is likely that this was not common in antiquity.

Hieroglyphic writing started at the beginning of the third millennium BC. It developed, like cuneiform, from pictographs, to become phonetic in its full development. A very early example is the Narmer Palette (figure 125). This shows an Egyptian army defeating enemies (Egyptian defeats never seem to occur!). The palette has pictographs and also phonetic writing of names and titles, and so is of especial interest.

It is possible that sound values were first given to pictograms by a process akin to punning. Proper names, such as the names of rulers, could not be represented pictorially. But some names can be presented as pun-pictures (for example, names like Haycraft).

Hieroglyphic writing is really a double script, for each idea is represented both by a pictogram and also by a

122 *left*. Early pictographs. The drawings started as cartoon representations, becoming more 'abstract' with the development of the written language.

123 *centre*. Early Chinese pictographs. They were remarkably similar to early Egyptian symbols, though independently invented. In both cases they were cartoons of common objects.

124 *right*. Early cuneiform pictographs, from Mesopotamia.

139

125. The Narmer Palette, from Upper Egypt. This is one of the earliest examples of Egyptian writing and demonstrates how the stylised pictographs emerged from directly informative drawings, grouped to make a story.

phonogram. The pictograms remain largely self-explanatory cartoon drawings, while the phonograms can only be understood by knowing the spoken language.

Determinatives were used, to avoid as far as possible the ambiguity inherent in using but a few hundred pictograms to represent a great variety of objects, situations and ideas.

The early history of other ancient (and primitive modern) languages shows this same development from pictographs representing objects and classes of objects to abstract ideas relating to these objects, and to a written grammar associated with the particular spoken language in use. The phonetic units may be syllabic symbols, as in hieroglyphic Egyptian, or they may be alphabetic letters as in European languages. The alphabet – surely among the greatest inventions of man – allows about thirty symbols to represent the most subtle thoughts of which we are capable. It gives, in the permissible arrangements of the alphabetic symbols, a kind of mathematics of meaning.

The Egyptian hieroglyphic language, and the Minoan scripts found on the island of Crete, dating from the twenty-eighth century B C (becoming picturegrams by about 2000 B C), as well as the 4000-year-old Chinese script, are examples of successful language scripts in which the units are words and syllables rather than alphabetic letters. They are less convenient, but perhaps have certain advantages.

We are familiar with how ideas are expressed in an alphabetic language, such as English, where the original pictograms are echoed from the very distant past in the letter symbols but have no more than a historical significance. How were thoughts expressed in the ancient picture languages, such as Egyptian hieroglyphics?

Some of the hieroglyphic symbols remain, for the 4,000-year life of the language, simple pictures of what is represented. Here are some examples:

snake   🐍   pregnant woman   𓀠

Then there are symbols used for abstract concepts, such as:

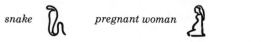

motion   ∧   strength   ⌣⌣   light or time   ☉

These are obviously abstractions from particular objects – for example legs and arms associated with movement and strength. We also find symbols representing still more abstract ideas, sometimes based on mystical or magic associations, such as:

evil 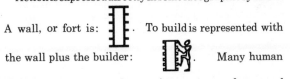.

Almost every Egyptian word is followed by an ideographic sign, which is either a picture of the object or a symbol representing a more general class. For example, the word

ah, an ox, may be written or , the

sign being the picture of the animal and the

, a hide, being the class symbol for quadrupeds.

This sign is a determinative, establishing the general class to which the symbol of the ox is to belong. A sign, such as the picture of the ox, may also be used not to represent any object but as a phonetic symbol, representing a sound of the spoken language.

Action is expressed directly in some ideographic symbols.

A wall, or fort is: . To build is represented with

the wall plus the builder: . Many human

actions are represented as action postures of men and women. Here are some examples: *to adore or to reverence*

 *to sing*  *a defeat*

to be buried or embalmed .

Parts of the body are used as verbs: *to see* or *to take notice*

of  *to weep* . Animals and parts

of animals or flowers are also used as verbs, often with related though multiple meanings: *to fly* or *fly away*

 *to stop*  *joy* .

One of the most serious limitations of pictures for communicating ideas is the difficulty of indicating that something is *not* the case. Symbols for logical relations are often omitted, and probably were developed gradually. There is however a frequently occurring symbol for 'not',

representing graphically a gesture of the arms .

Other logical relations are written: *if* ,

141

and ▨ , *or* ▨

For an example of a negation, we may take the sentence:

'I know him not' ▨ *em rekh-y su.*

This sign for negation is derived from a gesture, a parting of the hands. It could be the original of our own mathematical sign for negative '—'.

The invention of *determinatives* in the hieroglyphic language was a key invention, allowing picture-symbols to be read unambiguously and allowing picture-language to represent things which could not be represented directly as pictures. An especially interesting determinative is the picture-sign for a papyrus roll. It is written:

▨. This is a determinative sign for the abstract – that which cannot be pictured, only written or spoken. In the earliest periods numbers were written by duplicating the sign of the object. Thus two eyes would be written:

▨

Special signs were however developed for numbers:

I	units	𝟙	thousands
∩	tens	⌐	tens of thousands
℮	hundreds	↘	hundreds of thousands

The number 11,549 would be written:

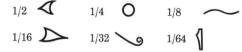

Fractions were written in several ways. The ancient system, which continued in use for land or corn was given by halving and is most curious. The following fractions could be written:

1/2 ◁   1/4 ○   1/8 ～

1/16 ▷   1/32 ↘   1/64 〈

These symbols formed part of an eye: the right eye of Horus, the Sun. In an ancient myth, no doubt representing the fight between day and night, evil and good, the evil god Seth attacked and tore to pieces the eye of Horus. Thoth, the god of learning, reason and justice, put the pieces together again to make the 'sound eye of Horus'. Possibly the fragmenting and mending of the sun-eye was suggested by partial loss of the sun in eclipses. At any rate, the signs for the fractions together form the eye of the god:

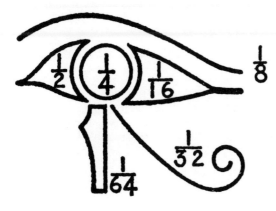

126. The Eye of Horus, divided into the signs for the fractions. This follows an ancient myth in which the Eye (the sun) was torn to pieces by the God of Darkness, to be mended by the God of Learning, Thoth.

This is an extremely sketchy account of a topic which would surely repay a great deal of careful research – just how what is known of the early history of written languages can reflect and illuminate the early development of human thinking, especially if as we have supposed thinking emerges from seeing. At first glance – and this is no more – it emerges that the first written languages started as pictures of things which could be directly represented as pictures. We may call these 'noun-pictures'. The addition of signs used to indicate the generality of noun-pictures – determinatives – made it possible to convey more abstract ideas, the determinatives helping to avoid the ambiguity which must follow by using the same symbol in different ways. As symbols were used for more and more abstract concepts, the ambiguity problem must have grown worse and the system of determinatives became essential. Together with this, the picture-symbols became linked with speech sounds and were used to represent spoken words. The original picture-significance was then lost, and it is impossible to guess the meaning of hieroglyphics from the picture-symbols of the words. Where possible, however, the meaning is also given in the original pictogram form – and this can often be read by the untutored eye.

To our eyes the lively picture-symbols are evocative in the extreme: re-creating the lives and the thoughts of a very early civilisation. They are gone but they speak to us from the past. We see, pictured, their object-hypotheses – their units of seeing and thinking – their intelligent eyes.

Language – a mental tool

One of the most puzzling mysteries of biology is the fact that only man has language. True, many animals can signal danger: bees can signal not only the presence, but also the direction and approximate distance of nectar. Animals certainly have emotive cries and can affect one another's behaviour with threat or entreaty. But it seems that no animal but man has the ability to represent the steps of an argument with an ordered sequence of signs, verbal or written.

It is also true that no animal can draw noun-like pictures. Desmond Morris has found that apes will paint various rather unstructured patterns, but never recognisable pictures of objects. The earliest such pictures are the cave paintings of man.

It seems that the ability to accept certain shapes as symbols is uniquely human. One might think that a sufficient explanation for why it is that we alone have language is that our brains are larger than other brains, but this may not be quite correct. There is a rare genetic abnormality – nanocephalic dwarfism – in which the adult height is as little as 23 in. and yet the body has approximately normal proportions. The brain is greatly reduced in size – being smaller than the brain of a normal chimpanzee. It is likely that the number of brain cells is reduced, since the size and density appear normal. Yet nanocephalic dwarfs, with their greatly reduced brains, can use language. They can speak and understand at least as well as a five-year-old child, which is far beyond the language skill of a chimpanzee. What does, perhaps, seem to be important is the unique laterality of the human brain. For most people the left cerebral hemisphere becomes dominant, at about the age when language becomes established. People who develop right-hemisphere dominance often have some language difficulty. In so far as is known, cerebral dominance is unique to the human brain. Its significance is not understood, but it is generally agreed that regions of the left hemisphere are uniquely important to language. It has also been suggested that damage to the left hemisphere reduces man to something very like the ape. A man so damaged can still see, and behave appropriately to normal objects, but he may lose the uniquely human ability to use symbols effectively when the left hemisphere is damaged. It seems that it is something about the particular structure rather than about the size of the human brain which is vital for appreciating symbols and using language.

It is vital to remember that visual perception – in the sense of behaving appropriately to non-visual as well as directly to visual features of objects – occurs in creatures far removed from man down the evolutionary scale. Also, fairly sophisticated problem-solving, of what we might call an 'intellectual' kind, is possible for animals at about the evolutionary rung of dogs, cats and the laboratory rat. Rats display 'insight' in certain laboratory maze-learning situations. It is well established that a rat will generally adopt the shortest of alternative paths through a maze. If then the shortest path is blocked, he will select the next shortest available route, without having to re-explore and relearn the maze. This seems to imply (together with other evidence, such as a tendency for errors during maze learning to occur in the direction of the goal) that some kind of internal 'map' of the maze is built up during learning and used for guiding behaviour.

It has been shown that rats will adopt and test simple hypotheses. In the classical experiment, the rats were presented with a series of closed doors under each of which was a light. Only one light would be switched on at a time, and all the doors except one were locked. The rat had to jump at a door: if it was the unlocked door he passed through and was rewarded with food. If it was a wrong door, locked, then he fell down and had to start again. The only clue to which was the unlocked door was the relative position of the light. It could be the door to the right of the light, or the door above the light, or any other relation. In this situation, the rats would try a 'hypothesis' such as that it was the door to the right of the light, wherever the light appeared, and then if after several trials this failed, they would try another hypothesis until finally they mastered the situation. The point is, they did not try any random combination of positions of doors and lights: they worked through and tested specific hypotheses quite systematically (Krechevsky, 1935).

Animals can apply learned skills to somewhat different situations. In other words, 'transfer of training' allows them to use past experience for somewhat novel present situations.

It is however true that 'reasoning' is extremely limited in animals, compared to the abilities of children at and over language-using age.

Unfortunately it is not known whether it is *language itself* which confers such benefit on man, or whether it is *ability to use language* which is the key to the situation. (The various cases of babies brought up by wolves, and so denied early experience of language, are unsatisfactory. The babies may be mentally deficient, for various reasons: we should in any case expect such a bizarre early environment to produce other losses.)

Words have always occupied the attention of philosophers, no doubt because they are the tools of philosophy. In early thought, names of objects are regarded as characteristics of the objects, not labels attached to them by men. This is the view of children, as Piaget has shown, and it was also the view of Aristotle, who regarded words as part of the essence of things. But this is very far from any modern view of language.

It is clear to us that words are applied to objects, situations, values and concepts by us. 'In the beginning was the word' is for us poetry; we cannot accept this order for the origin of language. It is however quite generally believed by linguists that there may be aspects of language which are innate. Although names for objects are in a sense arbitrary, there is evidence for believing that languages have common structural features which reflect aspects of the brain's essential information-processing procedure. If this is so, study of the way the brain is organised functionally should be relevant to understanding language; while the study of language structure may reveal something of the way the brain functions.

We have taken the view that perception is prototype thinking. Concepts started as hypotheses of the surrounding world, at first tied to objects and classes of objects: later to float free of sensory control, to allow abstract thought and the use of symbols.

Lenneberg says (in *The Biological Foundation of Language*):

Concepts are superimpositions upon the physically given; they are modes of ordering or dealing with sensory data. They are not so much the product of man's cognition, but conceptualisation is the cognitive process itself. Although this process is not peculiar to man . . . man has developed the behavioural peculiarity of attaching words to certain types of concept formation.

Perception in animals involves the active building of concepts, but we alone can name our concepts and handle the names in a language. We can use our language to tag

146

and compare our concepts, and explicitly to put them to the tests of observation and challenge from other people. Through language people can pit their concepts against each other, to check against error and by mutual addition make up deficiencies in individual experience and understanding. We see this in its most refined form in teaching. Written and spoken language allows us to put our concepts in series and in parallel; through language concepts extend beyond the individual. Judging from the early history of written languages (for example Egyptian hieroglyphics), the process started by drawing pictures by selecting relevant details of objects and situations. As the concepts became more abstract and could be arranged in more subtle ways the pictures, as such, became inadequate. They evolved into formal symbols, in a structured language. We can still see embalmed in written language its simple picture origins.

Thought is *primarily* concerned with the properties and potentialities of objects, for it is these that are important for survival. Above all, thought is concerned with predicting the immediate future, and if necessary changing it to avoid disaster or gain reward. It is interesting that the content and subject-matter of the early languages is not philosophy or abstract speculation; but lists of possessions, accounts of victories in war and elaborate funeral observances for the dead. The preoccupation of the Egyptians with death seems concerned rather with the hope of continuing life's pleasures than any curiosity over the nature of life. Sir Alan Gardner, in his great *Egyptian Grammar*, writes (page 3):

The most striking feature of Egyptian in all its stages is its concrete realism, *its preoccupation with exterior objects ... Subtleties of thought such as are implied in 'might', 'should', 'can', 'hardly', as well as such abstractions as 'cause', 'motive', 'duty', belong to a later stage of linguistic development. ... Despite the reputation for philosophic wisdom attributed to the Egyptians by the Greeks, no people has ever shown itself more averse from speculation or more wholeheartedly devoted to material interests.*

Granted that, with the development of written language, thinking gradually became abstract, freed from perceptual situations, we can only speculate that the symbols were necessary for the thought; that the symbols freed the brain from the tyranny of sensory perception. One might say that this is the role of both artist and scientist.

It is possible to estimate the importance of a tool, or an aid of any kind, by noting the improvement that it confers. The benefit of a new machine in a factory is estimated by the increased output. Now if the output is very much

127–132. Modern pictographs. These international signs can be understood apart from formal language; their meaning is seen from our shared experience of objects rather than from sign-conventions; just as in the first written languages.

increased, it is clear that the machine it replaced, or aided, must have been correspondingly inefficient. It is therefore possible not only to estimate the efficiency of the new machine but also to deduce a good deal about what it replaces or augments. In human terms, a carpenter without chisels, saws or drills, cannot even begin. So we would know at once (a Martian could deduce it) that men do not have limbs already equipped to chisel, saw or drill. We can now apply this argument to mental ability. It is well known that the simple *abacus* enormously improves the speed and reliability of human beings at adding numbers. It follows that the brain must be inefficient at holding numbers in short-term store, and operating upon them with simple rules. We are so bad at arithmetic that a few beads on wires improve our efficiency many times, while slow-acting geared adding machines are better than brains. This opens the way to supposing that symbols and positional rules – written languages – serve to make up deficiencies of our brains shared with other animals. Apart from symbols our brains are not too impressive.

The notion that the brain's processes of perception are similar to logical processes used for collecting and making sense of data in science, using hypotheses of various kinds suggested and tested by the data of human and instrumental observations, is attractive. Indeed, we can think of science as a kind of shared perception. Science makes great use of formal symbols of language and mathematics, and there are accepted types of argument. Making assumptions as clear as possible; stating the procedure used for making measurements; deriving conclusions from the assumptions and measurements as clearly as possible: these are all regarded as essential for good science. It has taken a very long time to emerge from myth and magic to such a formalised, and as it turns out powerful, approach to understanding and controlling nature.

We have encountered some facts suggesting that the perceptual system is far less 'rational'. For example, if conflicting information is presented down two or more sensory channels, we may experience a logical paradox. The scientist would regard a paradox due to conflict of data as a sure sign that something was wrong – perhaps with his instruments, or that he had made an error of calculation. At any rate, he would not allow an evident paradox to remain unchallenged. Not so for perception: in the autokinetic effect we see a light both moving and yet not changing its position. We get the same paradox in the after-effect of movement. With adaptation to heat with one hand, cold with the other, the same bowl of water is experienced as both hot and cold at the same time.

There could be a deep philosophical implication in this acceptance of perceptual paradoxes. If we have to learn about the world from the data given by the senses, then presumably we have to learn not only what is physically possible but also what is physically *impossible*. In other words, if we accept an empiricist philosophy, we should not expect physically or even logically impossible situations to be automatically rejected by the nervous system. What is impossible is not given *a priori* any more than truth is given before we discover it by 'rationalising' facts. We need experimental philosophy!

The eighteenth-century empiricist philosophers regarded perception as a passive process, whereas now we think of it as an active building and testing of hypotheses, which change to some extent throughout life. This means that we cannot, as they did, believe in raw data of perception and suppose that perceptually given 'facts' are solid bricks for basing all knowledge. All perception is theory-laden. Worse still, the perceptual hypotheses can differ from our most firmly held intellectual beliefs. We see this in the case of the distance of the moon: it is intellectually about a million times more distant than it appears. We see the sun moving across the sky though we know that it is the ground under us which is rotating with respect to the 'fixed' stars: so it is easier to *think* of the earth as rotating but easier to *see* it as the sun and the sky moving. Primitive beliefs are determined by how things are seen.

It is not difficult to demonstrate the fallibility of thinking based on perception, when the situation is beyond the range of sensory situations. We have all, as children, folded pieces of paper, and as adults we fold letters and newspapers every day. Imagine performing the following operation and try to visualise the result. In imagination take a sheet of tissue paper a few thousandths of an inch thick and as large as you like. Now fold it in half. Now fold it again, so that the double thickness becomes four thicknesses. Repeat this folding fifty times. Now, how thick is the folded paper? People generally give an answer between ½ in. and 3 ft. But the answer is, that the thickness of paper would be about the distance of the sun! It seems quite absurd that all we have to do to reach the sun is fold a sheet of tissue paper fifty times, and yet this is indeed so. The mathematical notion of physical quantities increasing by a power law evidently is not well represented in our perceptual models, and intuition then fails dramatically. Mathematically, we can see that 2^{50} is going to be a very large number. We need the power of symbols to extend our perceptual models of the world to cover cases beyond the range of direct experience. The error between the mathematically given answer of

100 million miles for the folded paper, and the perceptual intuitive answer of about 1 in. is about 6×10^{12}. This is an absurdly large discrepancy.

We see, then, that perceptual models can accept paradoxes, and be wildly in error when extrapolations beyond experienced situations are involved. This limitation can worry physicists in their work. Physical theories adopted up to the end of the nineteenth century were all compatible with, and no doubt directly derived from, perception of familar objects. Orbits could be thought of as like stones whirled round on a piece of string; atomic interactions as like billiard balls; the æther like a jelly, transmitting vibrations of light. It was when a few crucial experiments showed that the reality described by physicists in terms of how we see familiar objects led to paradoxes that the trouble began. Light had to be both waves *and* particles – but no objects are both. No change in the speed of light was detectable between the direction of movement of the Earth in one direction and a direction at right angles to this direction. But how could this be if light travels through a medium anything like what we know through sensory experience?

Twentieth-century physics has largely abandoned the ages-old perceptual models of reality. The essential concepts of quantum physics, and some of the concepts of relativity theory, have no counterpart in even the physicist's own perceptual models, and so he has great difficulty in thinking 'intuitively' in his subject. Partly for this reason mathematical formulation, and computer simulation, have become essential and dominate physics. This has led to a curious situation: the physicist in a sense cannot trust his own thought. He is reliant upon more or less accepted conventions of symbolic systems. They have taken physics and its insights away from the understanding of other scientists who are largely cut off from the thinking of the physicists – and yet it is the claim of the physicists to set the ground rules for the other sciences.

We can, perhaps, see this situation as a direct result of two specifically human accomplishments: the development of language and the development of measurement. Language, allowing logical and numerical relationships to be expressed without ambiguity, and measurement with instruments to check the accuracy and extend the range of the senses, are the two crucial developments which distinguish man from all other animals. They have allowed us to take the extraordinary step of developing accounts of the world quite different from the way we see it. So physicists live with their normal object-hypotheses and also with their often conflicting abstract symbolic accounts of reality. The first instruments made more precise what was already signalled to the brain from the senses. We can judge lengths and angles fairly well, but rulers and protractors give the added accuracy needed for even quite primitive technology. It would be extremely difficult to do the simplest carpentry and impossible to do joinery without these instrumental aids. In fact, the precision attained with even the simplest is quite surprising: the Great Pyramid was built from stone blocks cut with only millimetre errors. Already technology had started the divorce from human sensory limitations leading to theoretical physics, which in an important sense cannot be understood by anyone.

We see how mental constructs – at first used to guide behaviour in the absence of sensory information adequate for direct control – were externalised and made public: first in pictures then in symbols of increasing abstraction, including formal arrangements representing chains of logical argument and the very structure of thought. If thought itself is arrangements of neural circuits whose activities are representing concepts, we may think of language systems as extensions of brain activity; then writing is but a step towards autonomous thinking machines.

Present instruments detect and measure 'things' never represented to the brain by the senses. The great range of the electromagnetic spectrum was unknown, apart from heat and light, before instruments were available – radio receivers, infra-red photographic emulsions and screens sensitive to X-rays. They provide entirely new basic data; data available only to man, so that we are now even more separated from our biological origins. We can see the effects of this extension of basic data dramatically in the social history of astronomy.

Man must have made unaided observations of the night sky for many thousands of years. Some of these observations were probably recorded in various ways from the earliest times, leading to calendars and prediction of eclipses. (It has been suggested that Stonehenge was an astronomical computer for predicting eclipses.) The aids of simple scales and pointers in the form of astronomical quadrants (figure 134) provided data sufficiently accurate for mathematical models of planetary movements, in three-dimensional space, to be suggested and tested. The varying planetary distances were not available to direct measurement, but nevertheless the measurements that were available (especially those of Tycho Brahe) had sufficient accuracy to allow Kepler to formulate his three laws of planetary motion, which led directly to Newton's *Principia* and a mathematical account of the Universe. The 'bricks' of Newton's account are, however, still the forces and substances monitored directly by the senses. The Universe was still a collection of pushes and pulls, hardness, heat and shape. (The so-called 'secondary qualities', such as colour, had a doubtful status, because they seemed essentially attached to the *observer*, and so not quite objective: not quite 'out there'.)

The telescope allowed the pattern-recognition and object-perception powers of perception – developed biologically for objects on Earth – to be applied for the

133. An orrery is a physical model of selected features of the solar system. The movements of the planets are represented by spheres on wire driven by gears. There is a formal similarity to the planetary system which helps us to understand the solar system – provided we select what is appropriate. Models are a kind of cartoon-language. Just as the pictographs of ancient languages became ideograms for expressing complex ideas – finally expressed by purely abstract symbols as pictures become inadequate – so such models become restrictive. They give way to mathematical theories which cannot be represented by pictures or models. Perhaps thought in terms of the brain's perceptual hypotheses becomes inadequate as theories become more general and abstract.

first time to the features of the sun, moon and planets. Its light-gathering power revealed new objects; new stars and, most startling at the time, the system of moons circling round Jupiter. The 'imperfections' of the sunspots, and the mountains and shadows of the moon – not a burnished golden globe but all too Earth-like – shattered ancient preconceptions at a blow: most profoundly, by demonstrating the power of instruments and observations to counter philosophy based purely on perception. The simple fact that stars exist invisible to the unaided eye made it unlikely that the heavens are but a backcloth for the stage of human drama. This in turn threw doubt upon our role as the chief characters in the play – and whether there is a script or Script Writer for our parts.

It is indeed strange that the curved glasses of telescopes and microscopes should have so changed the image of man to himself. We are almost drop-outs from the Universe our glasses have revealed.

It is not difficult to guess in part how man started with a very personal view of the stars. Looking up at the sky

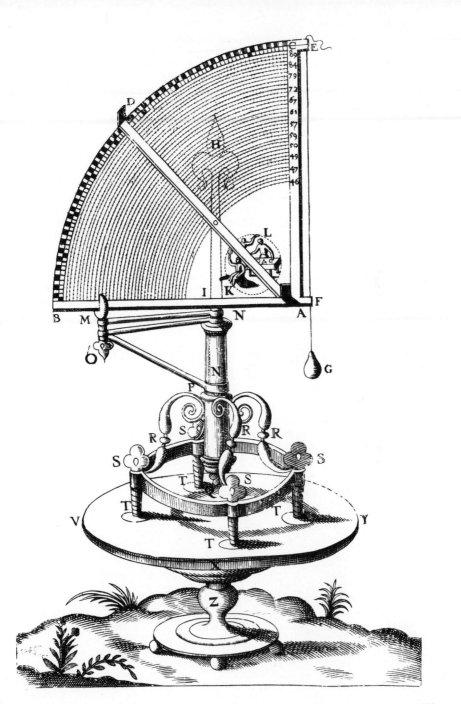

while walking or riding at night he would see the moon and stars apparently following his every movement. Of course we know that this is simply because they are so distant that there is no relative backward movement as we move forward. So in relation to the nearby objects on Earth, they seem to move with the traveller, sharing his every experience. But once the scale and the geometry are understood all this goes; all reason for a close personal association with the Universe (hence astrology) is lost; and we are either left out in the cold, rejected, or absorbed in the non-perceptual accounts of science.

The radio telescope has added non-sensory information about the stars. It is not an extension of any existing sense, but monitors quite new information bringing its own surprises; most recently the pulsars, transmitting bursts of radio energy at precisely equal intervals of about one second. We have to learn to live with non-sensory data, and the resulting non-perceptual concepts of physics. We are left with a question: how far are human brains capable of functioning with concepts detached from sensory experience? Our future depends upon the answer.

Seeing how things work

By looking at a machine, or a process, we can sometimes 'see' how it works. We are able to read function from structure.

People from a culture where machines are familiar can 'see' that a large cog or chain wheel will turn more slowly than a smaller one meshed with it. We can 'see' that a bicycle with a large rear wheel will go faster than a bicycle with a smaller rear wheel though both rotate at the same rate. It may not, however, be nearly so obvious why the bicycle stays upright – even if running downhill with no rider to control it. Engineers can 'see' the functional significance of the parts of quite complicated systems. It is very interesting to examine the mechanism of a clock (figure 135), and try to see the function of its

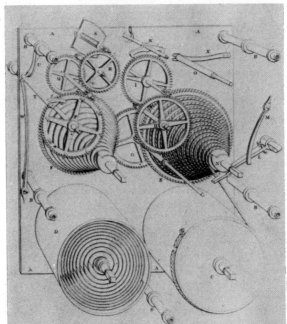

135. We can sometimes read from a drawing how something such as a mechanism works. This is a subtle matter, implying that we can read back the correlations made in perceptual learning of non-optical, physical properties of objects, from images. Originally these characteristics must have been associated by learning. Here we reverse the process, to understand physical function from drawings of structure. This drawing of a clock was used by Charles Babbage, in 1826, to illustrate how function can be 'read' from structure – but with limitations. He devised a special symbolism for showing the function of parts represented in drawings; to help him in designing the first computer.

wheels and springs and the escapement anchor with its cunningly shaped pallets without which the clock will not work. We may say that if we can do this, our object-hypotheses of these various parts are sufficiently general and precise to be used to describe – and explain – the functioning of the system. It is indeed sometimes possible to read function from structure using the richness of our object-hypotheses.

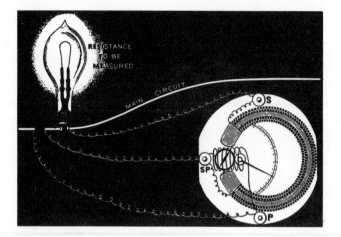

In mechanical systems, the spatial positions of the component parts and their shapes are vital to the functioning of the system. A clear picture of a mechanical system can be extremely informative, because pictures convey structural information (though with uncertainty as we have seen) and it is structure which is vital for mechanical understanding. But electronic systems – and here we may include neurological systems including brains – do not depend so much on the precise location of their parts, or on the shape of their components. A resistor or a condenser can be any of a wide variety of shapes and work as well. No doubt the same is true of nerve cells. In short, the kind of knowledge of structures which can be pictured does not give the same functional understanding of electronic or neural systems that it does of mechanical devices. Visual information, which has been so useful in the history of our own and of previous species for understanding the physical world of objects, is of less use for problems of science where physical structure is not the key to function.

Nevertheless, electronic engineers can 'read' a circuit diagram. They can see from the components and their

136. An early (1884) drawing of a Wheatstone bridge circuit. Here we see the start of a modern hieroglyphics. At this stage the components are drawn as they appear, without emphasis on their functional characteristics.

connections how the circuit works, in terms of the functional significance of the components.

The symbols used for electronics since the beginning of this century parallel the development of the pictograms of ancient languages. At first the symbols were realistic drawings of the components. Within a few years the electronic 'pictograms' became simpler: the emphasis was placed on the functionally important features of the

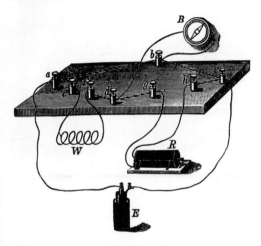

components, while the outward shapes were lost. The symbols pictured their functional significance. Each symbol is a kind of abstract cartoon. Figures 136–9 show some of the development of the symbols used in circuit diagrams, over fifty years of rapid development.

137. A later (1890) drawing of a Wheatstone bridge circuit. This is somewhat more stylised, with emphasis on the functional features of the components.

To understand the present symbols in electronics it is essential to know something of the fundamental processes of electronics. Its logic must be understood. The symbols are words in a language – a language adapted to express certain kinds of interacting processes.

We may say that verbal languages and mathematics, and specialised 'languages' such as the formal use of symbols in electronics, allow us to deduce the consequences of hypothetical actions in realms where sensory experience does not apply and cannot be pictured directly.

Symbols have come to represent not merely physical structures which can be represented, if imperfectly, by pictures: symbols can represent structures in abstract realms of thought where the mechanics of objects may be of little concern.

Like any other functioning system the brain may be considered in many different ways. There is not necessarily any one best kind of description of a social, an economic or an engineering system. The same is true of descriptions of the brain and its functions. Its structures, as seen by the naked eye or the light or electron microscope, are important for answering some functional questions. Classification of its various component cells, and their number or relative numbers in each region, may be important, as well as the connections between

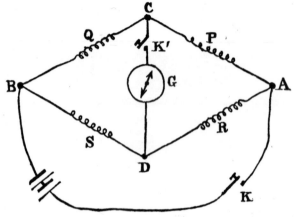

138. A still later (1898) drawing of a Wheatstone Bridge circuit. By now the components are not drawn as they appear: they are drawn with conventionalised symbols, in which function is revealed to the initiated. But such symbols are meaningless to those with no understanding of – in this case – electrical theory. Symbols only have meaning for those who share perceptual hypotheses, or abstract theories.

them. Structural descriptions are also important for electronic circuits – when the layout and connections determine the functioning of the system. Features are important which when changed change the behaviour of the system. On this count the colours, and generally the shapes, of components are unimportant: if they are changed the input-output characteristics are unaffected. By finding out what changes do occur, we can often decide which features are important for understanding a system. It should, however, be added that when *no* change of function occurs with a change of structure we cannot always assume this structure to be unimportant – for the system may adapt to the local change. Or other components may take over the function of parts that have been changed or removed. We should not then conclude that these parts had no function, though this is how it might appear. It is very difficult to discover how a system functions by removing or modifying parts and noting what happens in cases where there is no clear relation between structure and function.

This is a pitfall for neurology. We have to use symbols to represent function. Symbols become substitutes for the original. They retain what is relevant and reveal causal or other relationships. The symbolic system is an idealisation of the original; and since it is a simplification it cannot describe all the properties of the original. But it is hardly going too far to say that the progress of the physical sciences *is* the substitution of descriptions of objects and phenomena by formal abstract symbolic systems. We appear to be on the brink of being able to think use-

139. This drawing, from an 1890 handbook on electricity, shows three stages of the convention of symbols in a single drawing; the levels of abstraction perhaps reflecting the knowledge of each feature. The battery (well under-stood at that time) is shown with a *function* symbol based on its plates; the telephones are shown as *structures*, with no emphasis of what is functionally important. The terminals where the wires are attached are shown with a detail which appears to us comic. The lady and gentleman are shown in structural surface detail. Perhaps, in a later century, people will be represented not by portraits, but by symbols representing the logic networks and behaviour-bias functions of their nervous systems. Meanwhile, the human face remains the interface for visual communication. We have to read the state of another's mind from characteristic features which are far removed from the brain's function and which are most inadequate for predicting behaviour. As an interface, the face leaves much to be desired.

fully about brain function in this way, which has been so successful in the physical sciences.

Regarding the brain as a device, however complicated and however unknown, makes it possible to classify brain research in the terms of the kinds of explanation and descriptions used for engineering systems. It goes something like this:

Biological	Physical
1 Anatomy and histology	Mechanical description, using shapes.
2 Physiology	Functional relations of components (e.g. electronics) and the physical principles by which the components work.
3 Psychology	Logic of information-handling – 'software'.

159

These are all very different accounts of functional systems. It is very important to recognise how difficult it is to move from one kind of description to another without making terrible mistakes. The kinds of observations which are appropriate for each, and the logic of these symbolic systems are very different. Indeed, the gap between 'consciousness' and information-processing is perhaps no greater than the gaps between these categories. We are just more used to making such remarks as: 'The brain is conscious.'

It is these vital functional properties of the components and their interactions which are represented by the symbols of circuit diagrams. These symbols have become a special language to represent the principles and practice of electronic systems. They are indeed a new kind of hieroglyphic language. We need similar languages for brain function.

Logic
Philosophers divide logical arguments into two broad, essentially different, classes: *inductive* and *deductive* arguments.

It is tempting to suppose that object-hypotheses are derived by logical *inductions* while the arrangements of the symbols of language represent logical *deduction*.

The distinction between induction and deduction is both basic to logic and vital to further consideration of the relation between perception and thinking.

The philosopher R.B.Braithwaite, describes induction as: 'the inference of an empirical generalisation from its instances, or of a scientific hypothesis from empirical evidence for it' (*Scientific Explanation*, 1949). Inductions are generalisations of instances. A classical example of an inductive prediction is: 'All swans so far observed have been white: so the next swan that we see will be white.' A general prediction of the same inductive form is: 'All swans so far observed have been white: so *all* swans observed in the future will be white.' This happens to be an example chosen by Aristotle. By a strange and illuminating chance it turned out, some 2000 years later, that this classical inductive generalisation was false. Black swans were discovered, in Australia! Now if the argument had been framed in a *deductive* way it could not have been refuted. If 'white' had been used as a defining characteristic of 'swan', then the Australian discovery of black birds otherwise looking like swans could not have refuted the argument, because black swan-like birds could not have been included in the class of objects 'swans'. Thus the *induction* would be refuted, but the *deduction* would not be refuted by the new observation. Facts cannot refute deductions. They can only suggest that a given deduction is not applicable to the world as we find it.

If the premises of a valid deductive argument are true then the conclusion *must* be true. To take an example from arithmetic: if there are eight chairs in the dining-room and two chairs in the kitchen, then there must be ten chairs altogether. But if the premises are wrong, then although the conclusion will be factually incorrect the deduction is still sound and is not challenged. Deductive arguments cannot be refuted by facts: what can be refuted are the premises used for the deductive argument. An improbable or impossible conclusion makes us examine the premises more closely and this may well lead to the correction of the premises.

A way of deciding whether a given argument is inductive or deductive is to consider the premises in association with the contradictory of the conclusion. If the argument is *deductive* in form, then the contradictory of the conclusion will be logically incompatible with the premises. If it is *inductive* they will not be logically incompatible, though the statement may be extremely unlikely. If a bird cannot be said to be a swan unless it is white – because we are accepting 'white' as a defining characteristic of 'swan' – then to say: 'I have seen a non-white swan' is logically impossible. By seeing that it is *logically* impossible, we at once know that we were speaking in a deductive manner. We know that we were taking 'white' as a defining criterion of 'swan'. If, on the other hand, we were not taking 'white' as a defining characteristic then to say, 'I have seen a non-white (black) swan' is not logically impossible, though it may be – and before the discovery of Australia was – extremely unlikely.

Certainty in this sense is no part of observation. It cannot be given by perception. Any individual perception can be in error and no generalisation based on however many observations can be *logically* certain.

There is something very odd indeed about the status of deductive arguments. Deduction requires a formal symbolic language. We may say that deduction is non-biological – for there cannot have been deduction before there was formal language. It is most tempting to suppose that the kind of problem-solving used in perceptual brain processes is *inductive*, while the problem-solving used for abstract thinking and communication and calculation is essentially *deductive*. On this view deduction would be limited to the human brain, for we alone have formal language. It may also apply to computers which follow the formal rules of a language. Conceivably a computer could develop its own formal language, unaided by us. We might then say that it followed (or violated) its own type of deductive argument.

It seems clear that since perception is not limited to the human species, though we alone have formal languages, *perceptual processes cannot be essentially deductive*. We must therefore think of them as *inductive*.

This makes the fact that we can experience perceptual paradoxes more reasonable: evidently the perceptual system does not apply deductive-type checks on its conclusions.

We have regarded perception as a matter of building up and testing hypotheses. Hypotheses are also the end result and goals of science. It seems, though, that the logical structure of scientific and perceptual hypotheses are different. The hypotheses of formalised science are deductive, while perceptual hypotheses are essentially inductive. It is the incredible invention of deductive thinking (first from pictures to symbols, then to their formal arrangements in language) which has given unique power to the human brain: allowing us to transcend our biological origin.

Brain function

The brain makes sense of the world by making predictions. It is hardly misleading to call it a computer. Is it anything like man-made computers? If so, which kind of computer, if any, is it most like? Computers are commonly divided into two classes: analogue and digital. (Or they may be a mixture, when they are called 'hybrid'.) Now if we do consider the brain as a kind of computer, it is worth asking: 'Is it analogue or digital?'

To discuss this we must be clear of the distinction. Curiously enough, computer engineers seem to have given far less thought to their distinction than the philosophers have to their induction/deduction distinction. The computer distinction is generally made in terms of the kind of engineering system used: but I think this masks a much deeper and more important distinction, which is worth making as clear as possible.

In the first place, it is sometimes said that analogue computers work continuously – smoothly – while digital machines work in discrete steps. This would be an engineering distinction. But surely it will not do as a *defining* difference. Consider a slide rule. This is regarded as an analogue computer. A cursor is moved along a set of parallel scales, and the answer is read off by relating one scale with another for a given position. The cursor moves smoothly; it can be placed at any position of one scale for the answer to be read off from another. But suppose we put 'click stops' on the slide – perhaps to favour certain values for a special use of the rule. Would we then call it a digital computer? This seems most unlikely. Consider now the size of steps on the rule, or other such device. No mechanisms are perfectly smooth, but 'micro' irregularities or jerkiness can hardly make an 'analogue' system 'digital'. Surely the point is that the steps in digital systems must represent something. *They represent logical operations.*

The word 'calculate' comes from the Latin word for 'pebble'. It indicated how mathematical operations could be represented or performed by moving beads or pebbles in allowed ways. The moves in the 'game' represent mathematical or logical operations. It seems that digital devices work in steps just because symbolic languages work in steps. But analogue systems can represent functions directly, without analysis or formal statement, and give answers without going through the stepped operations of a calculation, and so can be continuous.

Analogue devices can work very fast, because they arrive at an answer by a direct route. Their accuracy is limited though they seldom make gross errors. Digital devices can work with any required accuracy, but they are slow compared with the rate of their internal operations and may make large errors. Most important, they require analytical schemes, calculi and sets of formal rules – algorithms. Now it is important to note that a 'digital computer' can be programmed to work as an analogue system. The difference between them, then, is not basically an engineering but a *logical* distinction. In practice there are engineering differences in computers designed to work in an analogue or digital manner, but these differences are essentially contingent – they merely reflect engineering convenience.

Returning to the brain, we should frame our question 'Is the brain analogue or digital?' in terms not of its visible structure but of whether or not it follows formal rules for arriving at answers.

We know that the kinds of rules we are considering demand a formal language; but we also know that perception occurs in animals, who have not the capacity for handling formal language. So we are forced to the conclusion that the brain is biologically an analogue system. With the development – or invention – of language man's biologically analogue brain can work in a digital mode. This is so remarkable that we can hardly begin to understand it.

It seems that symbols – originally pictures of familiar things and situations – became more abstract and were used with rules to represent formal structures of language and logic. They served the analogue brain by allowing it to take on fleeting stable states, necessary for representing the steps of deductive argument and computation. Words became the beads of our internal abacus; to confer on the human brain the alien power of deductive thought.

There is a somewhat different and perhaps more useful way of putting this. Consider the notion of *restraints*. There can be *physical restraints* and there can be *symbolic restraints*. The moves of the counters or pieces of a game such as chess are limited by symbolic restraints. Machines, until the invention of digital computers, functioned according to internal physical restraints imposed by levers, guides, wheels, push-rods, bearings and so on. The art of mechanical engineering is to impose appropriate and precise restraints while minimising impeding friction. Clockmakers were for several centuries the pioneers. The first calculating machines were arrangements of geared wheels built essentially like clocks, except that the machines could be set appropriately to particular situations – that is, to solve particular problems by mimicking symbolic restraints with their mechanisms. Once set up, the problem was solved by the machine following the mechanical restraints on its components as built in by its maker. The way the machine was set up was, however, not determined by its mechanical constraints but by the logic of the problem and the way it was formulated. Computer programmers speak of 'hardware' and 'software'. The hardware is the machine itself, in which the operations are determined by physical restraints, while the software is the symbolic statement of the problem and the operations required for solving it, which are followed by the machine. The software presents symbolic structure in terms of the physical restraints of the machine: for example that its components work in 'all-or-none' steps.

Software programmes are written in special computer 'languages'. A computer language must be compatible with the design of computer in use and it must be appropriate to the general kind of problem to be solved. There is some flexibility here; some computer languages are for special purposes, but others can be used conveniently for numerical or sorting and classifying problems.

To return to human perception and language. We may consider these two kinds of restraint in terms of brain function: Is thought guided by physical or by symbolic restraints? Symbolic restraints will not be imposed by the structure of the brain *per se*, but by the structure of the language and logic in use. By 'language' we may be talking about normal spoken language, or some special language such as a mathematics or a formal logic. Some logicians such as George Boole in the nineteenth century spoke of logic as the 'Laws of Thought', believing that logic was basic brain function represented by their symbols and rules. Other logicians have held that logical rules are essentially independent of brain function, but that they can control its function when required, much as software controls a computer.

What about the structure of normal language? The study of linguistics has recently made a dramatic advance, largely through the work of the American linguistic philosopher Noam Chomsky. Chomsky argues that natural languages have 'surface' and 'deep' structure. By surface structure he means the accepted rules of sentence construction. 'Bill has gone into the town to meet Mary' is an acceptable sentence. Suppose we introduce words of unknown meaning, it could still be a sentence of acceptable and recognisable surface structure of the English language. For example: 'Bill has ronked the tift to pleek plook.' We do not know what this means, but it can be parsed as an English sentence. In fact, the British linguist James Thorne has shown that sentences can be parsed by computer, though the computer does not 'know' the meaning of the words.

There is no limit to the number of sentences that can be constructed in a language. The rules of grammar allow any number of new sentences to be generated, and to be recognised, as sentences. Now to consider deep structure. Deep structure involves meaning. To appreciate the deep structure of a sentence we must know the meaning of the words in the sentence. This is seen most clearly by considering an ambiguous sentence. Here a single surface structure may represent alternative deep structures. For example: 'What upset Bill was looking at Mary.' This sentence has two very different meanings. It is a linguistic equivalent of the Necker cube. In both cases, the same input has alternative acceptable meanings. The deep structure, surely, represents hypothetical meanings allowed by the words and the surface structure in a sentence. This is very similar to the meaning given to retinal patterns in terms, ultimately, of the structure of the world of objects.

Chomsky regards the deep structure of language as biologically innate. This raises an immediate problem: has there been sufficient time for the deep structure to develop by evolutionary means? As language is at most but a few tens of thousands of years old this seems hardly possible, for surely appropriate changes to the brain could not have occurred in so short a time? What seems far more likely is that the deep structure of language has somehow developed from the much earlier perceptual structures of the object-hypotheses inherent in perception. Perhaps the invention of symbols was sufficient for this to take place – to externalise the structure of perception in language.

When used for abstract thought, and for planning future

action, object-hypotheses must be selected and combined independently of current sensory information. They must not be restrained by the present, except for immediate action. We may regard thought as 'games' played with object-hypotheses as counters, following in general the deep structure of language. To be appropriate for normal situations the rules must mirror the structure of the normal world of objects. We should surely expect special languages, with different deep structures, when thought is not restrained by the world of normal objects – languages of mathematics, electronics and perhaps art criticism and music.

Until recently, men in all cultures handled rather similar objects and used them for similar ends. But with the development of technology, for large parts of the day one man may be concerned with the queer properties of electronic circuits, another with magnetic fields and a third with zero gravity in which otherwise normal objects have inertial but no gravitational mass. These situations demand different skills: different ways of ordering, handling and seeing objects. As abstract and queer object properties become more important, we may expect languages to develop with deep structures to reflect the worlds which we discover and create: worlds which so far as we know are uniquely human. We are being cut off from the biological past which moulded the eyes and the brains and the speech of our ancestors. The Intelligent Eye is for the first time confronted with an essentially unpredictable future, where present object hypotheses are bound to fail. As we create so we must adapt to what we have created; the danger is that we may create a world beyond the restraints of our intelligence: a world we cannot see.

Stereoscopic projection and drawing in 3-D

Stereoscopic shadow-images

We have used plane projections of objects, given by casting shadows upon a flat screen. Shadow projection has been used by several experimenters concerned with perception, especially the American psychologist J.J.Gibson who has used the shadows cast by small light sources to remove the texture of objects, particularly to discover how far motion parallax can serve to indicate depth to the eye. The stereoscopic shadow projector, used for the stereo pictures of wire models in this book and for many of the experiments, was first described by the author in 1964 in a communication to *Nature*, reproduced below.

Stereoscopic shadow-images, by R.L.Gregory. (Reprinted from *Nature*, Vol. 203, No. 4952, pp. 1407–8, 1964.) (The reader is also referred to a full and clear mathematical account of this arrangement, published by Dr David N. Lee, in *Vision Research*, Vol. 8, Jan. 1969.)

The following simple arrangement makes it possible to project in stereoscopic depth, three-dimensional objects such as wire models of molecular or crystal structures. Small models may be presented enlarged in three dimensions, magnifications of ten or more times being possible. The optical arrangement consists of nothing but a pair of small bright light sources, separated horizontally by a few inches. The sources are placed behind 'Polaroid' filters, set at orientations differing by 90°. The point-polarised sources give a pair of shadow-images of an object, such as a wire model, placed between them and a silver screen. Alternatively, back-projection with a ground-glass screen can be used; but the screen must not de-polarise the light. When the shadows are viewed through crossed 'Polaroid' glasses, they are fused by the brain to form a single stereoscopic shadow-image lying in space.

There is no problem in explaining this effect. The point-sources cast shadows on the screen which are flat projections from slightly different positions. The shadows have the disparity of retinal images for eyes placed at the sources. The observer's brain fuses the two disparate shadows into a single stereoscopic shadow, looking incredibly like a real, but jet-black object. It lies in space either in front of or behind the screen, depending on which eye accepts which shadow. By using polaroids oriented at 45° from horizontal, the stereo shadow-image may be placed before or behind the screen simply by reversing the spectacles. Suitable light sources are miniature filament 12 v. 100 w.

tungsten-iodine lamps. The filaments should be oriented vertically, to give maximum horizontal resolution, which is important for giving maximum information of depth through disparity.

Magnification of the normal x- and y-axes is given simply by the ratio of the distance of the object from the lights to the object from the screen. Magnification in depth (z-axis) can be controlled by the horizontal separation of the lamps. In practice a magnification of at least $\times 10$ may be given; but the apparent size of the three-dimensional shadow-image is generally less than might be expected, because of perceptual size constancy.

When the object appears to be in space before the screen it looks smaller than when behind it, though the physical size is of course identical with either orientation of the polaroids. A further perceptual effect is most marked: when the observer moves his head, the stereo shadow-image appears to move with him, to slide across the screen, and rotate to follow the observer as though continuously aimed at him. This is because there is no motion parallax although the image lies perceptually in three dimensions: this corresponds to a normal object rotating to keep the same aspect to the observer though he moves. So he sees movement though his retinal images remain unchanged. When the observer moves away from the screen, the shadow-object does not shrink or lose its depth as might be expected; the reduced angle of convergence of the eyes evidently rescales the retinal disparity mechanism, so that a given disparity between the retinal images gives greater visual depth. This is indeed fortunate, for the shadow-image appears very similar over a wide range of distance, and so it can be used with effect in a large lecture hall for demonstrating suitable objects. They may be moved or touched by the demonstrator, which makes this a technique having advantages over photographic stereo projection. It is also a useful tool for investigating perception of depth while the observer is moving, and can form the basis of simulators for experiments on the guiding of aircraft and space vehicles.

This technique was devised for experiments supported by US Air Force grant *AF–EOAR* 63–93, monitored by the European Office, Office of Aerospace Research.

3-D drawing machines
It is possible to draw anaglyphs (colour-separated stereo pairs) by geometrical construction, though it is tedious. The principles are explained by D.W.Stover in *Stereograms* (Houghton Mifflin, 1966). As an aid, a pantograph may be used, for by moving the locating pivot sideways a horizontal shift is produced, corresponding to the pivot shift. But the pivot must be shifted by the correct amount for each depth, so this system is effectively limited to drawing in a series of planes lying at different visual distances. Among the best available 3-D drawings given by construction on a standard drawing-board are those by A.G.J. Davies in *Solid Geometry in 3-D* (Chatto and Windus, 1967).

There is no satisfactory book on stereoscopic photography and no 35 mm. stereo camera which is adequate to scientific work. Reflex focusing is not available; and it is necessary to separate the pair of negatives for separate mounting so that registration is lost. There should be a facility on the camera for effectively converging the lenses, as the eyes converge to fixate near objects. The most useful non-technical book on the subject is *Stereo Realist Manual*, by W.D.Morgan and H.M.Lester (Morgan and Lester, NY, 1954). It is illustrated with colour stereo pictures, converged with a plastic lenticular prism viewer. A more technical book is *The Theory of Stereoscopic Transmission and its Application to the Motion Picture*, by Raymond and Nigel Spottiswoode (University of California Press, 1953).

The author's first 3-D drawing machine (described on page 133) employed an optical system and electroluminescent image-retaining panels. It was first described at a Royal Institution Discourse and published in *Seeing in Depth* (*Proc. Roy. Instn.* **40**, No. 185, 1965). It is described in the British Patent 2748/66 but has not been fully described in print.

The main optical problems arise from (a) the limited depth of focus of the projection lenses, and (b) the reversals of the co-ordinates due to having to project the image of the drawing light on to the front of the image-retaining panels. Back-projection would simplify the design, for then the projection and viewing conditions would be symmetrical. Projecting and viewing from the front means that either a large optical beam splitter (half-silvered mirror) is required or the angle of projection and viewing must be non-normal, as in the design given. Non-normal projection introduces distortion which is compensated by viewing from the same angle the other side of the normal. It is vital for the spatial co-ordinates of the drawing light to correspond to the visual co-ordinates of the stereo image as seen by fusion of its pair of real images in the storage panels. In the present design, the movements of the drawing light to the panel are reversed in the x and y dimensions by the projection lenses, and have to be reversed by the viewing telescopes, whose magnification ($\times 4$) is designed just to resolve the grain of the storage panel. The large plane mirror lying optically between the projection light and the projection lenses is required to reverse the z (depth) co-ordinate – required because the projection is on the front of the panel and so approaches it when it should be receding. The plane mirror increases the optical path to the storage panel as the light is moved away from the observer, as though it were projecting on the back of the panel. But if it was accepted by the projection lenses directly, increase in optical path length would be given by moving the light *nearer* the observer, giving reversal between the z co-ordinates of his hand and his eyes.

This is certainly not the only possible optical system. Greater storage panel area can be used by adding deviating prisms or using a Wheatstone mirror stereoscope arrangement; but there are problems because longer focal length projection lenses are then required to cover the increased area, and this reduces the available range of movement of the drawing light before picture resolution is lost. The present design was developed largely empirically; to be simple, to use standard optical components and to give pictures which are adequate at least as a start to what may become an important aid to engineers, architects and others concerned to understand and represent structures.

A central theme of this book is that sensory information is used
to build up symbolic models of the world in the brain. We generally call these 'object-hypotheses' or more generally 'perceptual
hypotheses' implying that they are predictive. Also, perhaps the
word 'model' makes one think of a physical existing object in the
brain, but this of course would be highly misleading. They exist
only in the sense that a symbolic structure exists.

It is an interesting question: can we design machines which
build up in themselves 'models' or 'hypotheses' much as we
suppose is done by the brain? The following device is essentially
simple. It does not use a digital computer or a programme in the
accepted use of the word. What it does do is to build up a crude
internal representation – a disturbed photograph – which it then
uses to accept or reject incoming information according to
whether it matches its 'internal model'. The device has a very
practical application – to minimise the disturbance due to atmospheric turbulence, which seriously degenerates astronomical

140. The disturbance-rejecting camera *(left)* set up with the randomly agitated water bath *(right)* through which light from the object being photographed *(off picture to the right, not shown)* passes to the camera. The side covers of the apparatus have been removed for this photograph to show some of the internal mechanism. The photomultiplier *(hidden)* is in the left-hand vertical tube at the top of the apparatus; the Master Negative holder is at the top of the right-hand tube. The electromechanical actuators for the high-speed sampling shutter can be seen in the body of the instrument. They open the shutter at moments when the image is least disturbed. This apparatus and its electronics were built by my colleague Mr Steven Salter; the project is supported by the Paul Instrument Fund of the Royal Society.

pictures taken by earth-based telescopes. The first description of this idea was given in *Nature* in 1964. Since then we have built in my department a telescope camera, with support from the Paul Instrument Fund of the Royal Society, and have tested this on two large telescopes in America. We are now engaged on building a device to compensate the inevitable tracking errors over the rather long periods of time required for this image improvement.

The 'internal model' which is built up is itself a photograph, taken with a rather long exposure so that although it will be blurred by the disturbance every recorded feature will be in its correct position with reference to the other features of the photograph. This is a very simple form of internal model, for although it does represent a statistically correct representation – in which every feature is in its mean position though disturbed randomly by the atmospheric disturbance – it is of course limited to optical information, while we believe the brain's perceptual models to include non-optical information important for appropriate behaviour. In this instrument, the photograph is taken on a glass plate which, when exposed, is removed from the camera and processed, to form a transparent negative of the image. Meanwhile, the telescope continues to track the object: the moon, planet or whatever is being photographed. The photographic plate, which we will now call the 'master negative', is replaced in precisely the same position in the instrument, so that the object's image falls upon it.

Now every *dark* part of the master negative receives a *bright* region of the image, and vice-versa. If we look at the image through its own negative, we find that when they precisely coincide the negative cancels out the image so that very little light gets through. Any discrepancy is seen as a line of light where the bright parts of the image get through the transparent parts of the master negative. Mathematically, this arrangement gives an auto-correlation function. As the image changes, in this case due to atmospheric disturbance, it no longer corresponds precisely with the average position of each region. The errors can be detected by monitoring the light which gets through the master negative. The master negative represents not any arbitrary moment, but rather the average image as it is disturbed by the atmosphere. By monitoring the light which gets through, with a sensitive photomultiplier, we convert the moment-to-moment errors into discrepancy signals. The smaller the current from the photomultiplier the smaller the discrepancy between the image and the *average* image, which is correct, though

171

blurred with fine detail lost through turbulence. The discrepancy signals serve to actuate the high-speed shutter of a second camera, which (with an optical beam splitter) is receiving the fluctuating image. This shutter is allowed to open only when the photo-multiplier current is near its lowest: which is when the features of the image correspond most closely to their positions on the master negative. This second picture is very much better than the master negative – or any normal photograph – for this second picture is built up in a series of short exposures which only occur when the image is undisturbed.

Figure 141 shows a disturbed image passing through its own (long exposure) photographic negative. Disturbance is here least towards the right where image and negative cancel, giving blackness. The bright edges towards the left indicate mismatch, and would give a reject signal – closing the high speed shutter until the entire image is cancelled by the Master Negative, when further exposure takes place.

Figure 142 shows a highly disturbed picture of a model. Figure 143 shows the improvement given by the sampling system: it is taken through precisely the same disturbance as 142.

I am most grateful to my colleague Stephen Salter who has built the version of the camera shown in figure 140. The project is supported by the Paul Instrument Fund of the Royal Society, to whom I am most grateful for making this possible.

141. This photograph shows how the image appears when passing through its own negative. The image is cancelled, giving blackness, in the regions where the image and negative closely correspond. This fact is used to provide an electrical signal to the high-speed shutter in the apparatus that the image is undisturbed at that moment in time – causing the shutter to open to start building up the picture.

142. A highly disturbed picture, taken through the randomly agitated water bath. Practically all detail is lost by the disturbance.

143. The same test object as in figure 142 photographed through *exactly the same disturbance* but with the electronics switched on so that the camera only 'sees' the object during brief moments of minimal disturbance. This improvement is given by automatic selection of a total of two selected seconds out of ten minutes while the image is continually disturbed. The Master Negative used is the negative transparency of the print shown in figure 142. The apparatus has therefore not been provided with any information other than that it discovers for itself.

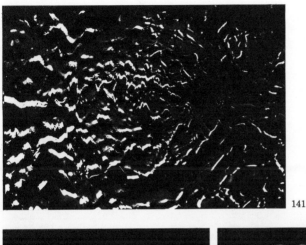

141

142

143

Notes

To make the book as easy to read as possible, references to specific papers and books have almost all been omitted from the text. The following notes are intended to make good the deficiency by providing references linked by comments related to the text. Since it is difficult to find bibliographical details hidden away in notes, the full references are also listed alphabetically at the end.

A central notion of this book is that perception is not a matter of sensory information giving perception and guiding behaviour directly, but rather that the perceptual system is a 'look up' system; in which sensory information is used to build gradually, and to select from, an internal repertoire of 'perceptual hypotheses' – which are the nearest we ever get to reality. This goes back at least to F.C.Bartlett in his classical *Remembering* (1932) and it is closely related to K.J.W.Craik's too little known *The Nature of Explanation* (1943). The origins and significance of the schema concept is discussed by R.C.Oldfield and O.L.Zangwill (1941–2) and (1942–3). See also M.D.Vernon (1955). Perhaps the thinking closest to the view of this book is S.J.Bruner's article 'On perceptual readiness' (1957). A recent book with a related approach is U.Neisser, *Cognitive Psychology* (1967). I believe that previous treatments (except perhaps Bruner) minimise the importance of prediction in perception – hence 'perceptual hypotheses'.

A major problem for an adequate theory of perception is how a system we know to have a low rate of information transmission in its peripheral channels can control complex behaviour in an ever-changing environment. The simple fact that we can recognise at a glance all manner of objects in a room is a major problem. We suggest that sensory information serves to select 'object-hypotheses', themselves built up from the wealth of past experience: this means that (a) only sufficient information for the selection needs to be available, or transmitted from the eye or other sense organs; (b) perception and behaviour can continue in the absence of all information while the selected hypotheses remain adequate to predict the immediate future, to control behaviour without serious error; (c) to allow, for example *non-optical* characteristics to be read from the purely *optical* retinal image. These characteristics seem to imply a 'look up' system; so basically we only need sufficient information to look up – and scale appropriately – our stored perceptual hypotheses of the external world. So much for our attempted type of solution. The background may be found in G.A.Miller (1956), F.Attneave (1954), D.E.Broadbent, *Perception and Communication* (1958) and C.Cherry, *On Human Communication* (1966). To consider the basis of information itself, regarded as a matter of selecting between possibilities (each with a finite and preferably known prior probability): C.E.Shannon and W.Weaver, *A Mathematical Theory of Communication* (1949) and J.R.Pierce, *Signals, Symbols and Noise* (1962).

1 Objects and pictures

Bishop Berkeley's philosophical position is most brilliantly presented by Bertrand Russell in his *History of Western Philosophy* (1946).

The evolution of vision is treated in most detail in G.L.Walls, *The Vertebrate Eye and its Adaptive Radiation* (1942). The first stages of vision through evolution are discussed by W.S.Duke-Elder, in *System of Ophthalmology* (1958), Vol. 1, and some general questions and speculations are raised in my article 'Origins of eyes and brains' (1967).

Visual reversible figures are discussed by the Danish psychologist Edgar Rubin in his *Synoplevede Figurer* (1915), but this has not been fully translated into English. Passages have been translated by Max Wertheimer and are to be found in Beardslee and Wertheimer (eds.), *Readings in Perception* (1958). I am indebted to this translation for the passages quoted.

There is a voluminous, but generally vague, literature of Gestalt Psychology. For a general account see W.Köhler, *Dynamics of Psychology* (1940), and K.Koffka, *Principles of Gestalt Psychology* (1935). The clearest account of the Gestalt notion of brain fields is W.Köhler, 'Physical Gestalten' (1920) tr. in Ellis (1938). The best account of perceptual organisation is M.Wertheimer, *Principles of Perceptual Organisation* (1923), tr. in Ellis (1938). A recent general book accepting a Gestalt point of view is J.E.Hochberg, *Perception* (1964), and an evaluation of its present status is J.E.Hochberg (1957).

The discovery that the frog's retina responds selectively to a small variety of specific visual features was first reported in J.Y.Lettvin, H.R.Maturana, W.Pitts and W.S.McCulloch (1959). The discovery that specific cells of the cat's visual cortex respond to specific shapes, or movement, was reported by D.H.Hubel and T.N.Wiesel (1962). This paper is followed by a long series in the *Journal of Physiology*. The discovery of the collection of information along cortical columns is reported by Hubel and Wiesel (1968).

The Ames distorted room and the other demonstrations are described in W.H.Ittelson, *The Ames Demonstrations in Perception* (1952) (revised with additions, 1968). See also his *Visual Space Perception* (1960). Ames himself wrote nothing systematic.

Helmholtz's discussion of 'unconscious inference' is to be found in his *Handbook of Physiological Optics*, now available as a Dover reprint (1963). This is invaluable to a student of perception.

2 The peculiarity of pictures

Among the first to discuss the nature of perceived space and the problems of pictures was the German philosopher and physicist, Ernst Mach, in *The Analysis of Sensations* (1886) and *Space and Geometry in the light of Physiological, Psychological, and Physical Inquiry* (1906).

The outstanding book from the point of view of the artist and art historian is E.H.Gombrich, *Art and Illusion* (1960). Gombrich revises his views on the importance of size and shape constancy and the activity of the perceptual system, in 'Visual

175

discovery through art' (1965). His views are discussed in a review by R. Wollheim, 'Art and Illusion' (1963). For the Gestalt point of view see R. Arnheim, *Art and Visual Perception* (1954) and 'Gestalt in Art' (1943).

The use of shadow projections as perceptual tools might almost be said to go back to Plato's flickering shadows in the cave. It has been used as an experimental tool, especially for studying the importance of motion parallax, by several workers including J. J. Gibson. Rotating wire shapes, viewed directly, have been used by F. J. Langdon; see 'The perception of a changing shape' (1951) and (1953). He provides a valuable discussion on constancy, with particular emphasis on Koffka's theory of strict size-distance invariance. The particular geometry of shadow projections can be used for measuring constancy by null methods: see R. L. Gregory, S. M. Antis and C. D. Shopland (1961). The use of a pair of point sources with cross-polarisation or colour filters, to give 3-D projection of objects, is described by Gregory in 'Stereoscopic Shadow-images' (1964). A full mathematical analysis of this has been given by D. Lee (1969).

Spontaneous depth reversal of skeleton figures was first described by a Swiss crystallographer, Necker, who noted the effect while drawing a crystal under his microscope; see L. A. Necker (1832).

Vision with stabilised retinal images has received considerable attention since the paper by R. M. Pritchard, W. Heron and D. O. Hebb (1960). They found that parts of figures appear and disappear spontaneously. It has been thought that reappearance is due to slippage of the optics giving stabilisation, but Evans has found similar spontaneous reappearances with structured flash after-images; see C. Evans (1965 and 1967). The investigation of visual depth ambiguity with simultaneous touch information is R. L. Gregory and C. D. Shopland (1964).

3 Paradoxical figures

M. C. Escher's paradoxical drawings are in *The Graphic Work of M. C. Escher*, London (1967). The impossible triangle and the impossible staircase pictures were first published in L. S. and R. Penrose (1958). (It seems better, however, to replace the term 'object' with 'picture' here: the distinction is important.) I am indebted to my research student, Stephen Young, for making the first impossible object. Insofar as I know, the first public appearance of an impossible object was at the R. I. Lectures (1967-8).

4 Distorting figures

Sensory adaptation and its physiological basis is described most clearly in Lord Adrian's classic books, *The Basis of Sensation* (1949) and *The Physical Background of Perception* (1947).

Adaptation to temperature, with the resulting paradoxical illusion, was given by Berkeley as one of his reasons for doubting the generally accepted validity of sensory experience.

Adaptation to movement was first described by Aristotle. It was first investigated in detail by A. Wohlmeguth, *On the After-effect of Seen Movement* (1911). A recent monograph on the subject is H. C. Holland, *The Spiral After-Effect* (1965). After-images are believed to be dependent on not only loss of photo-pigment resulting from bleaching out by the action of light, but also to change in the 'gain' of the retinal neural mechanisms; see W. A. H. Rushton (1962) and (1965). A recent discussion of the phenomenal aspects of after-images is J.L.Brown, 'Afterimages' in C.H.Graham (ed.), *Vision and Visual Perception* (1965). The physiological implications for colour vision are discussed in G.S.Brindley, *Physiology of the Retina and Visual Pathway* (1960).

The so-called Benham's top, or disk, has been rediscovered eight times. Its history is given in an entertaining paper: J.Cohen and D.Gordon, 'The Prévost-Fechner-Benham subjective colours' (1949). It turns out that the production of colour from movement or flicker was discovered by a French monk, Benedict Prévost, in 1826. It was rediscovered by Fechner in 1838, by John Smith in 1859, by Brewster in 1861, by F.J.Smith in 1881, by Hanney in 1881, by Stewart in 1887, by Charpentier in 1891 and, finally, by Benham (1894). (The variety of theories to account for these subjective colours varies from Fechner's – which is essentially the modern theory in terms of the time-constants of the receptor mechanisms – to John Smith who believed that the subjective colours proved the homogeneity of the aether, that they enable us to dispose of the different refrangibility of light rays, as taught by Newton, and a lot more of the same kind. This is an interesting example of what happens when 'subjective illusion' is confused with 'objective reality'. In this case, the French monk was clear on the matter and the scientist was confused.)

The very remarkable, newly discovered fact that after-effects of colour with movement and reversals in direction of movement of coloured stripes, is due to Celeste McCollough (1965).

Distortion figures were divided between the eyes by many investigators. The most important paper is P.Schiller and M.Wiener (1962) which gives the earlier references.

Among the first to attribute distortion to some kind of size-distance effect was A.Thiéry (1896), while R.Tausch (1954) considerably developed the notion, relating it to size-constancy. Such a theory does not, however, seem to work unless we suppose that (a) constancy is mediated by an active brain mechanism, giving perceptual size-change, and (b) that this can be set not only by apparent distances, but also directly by typical depth cues, even when these are countermanded by, for example, the surface texture of the illusion figure (Gregory, 1963, 1965, 1967, 1968), because the distortions occur though the figures are seen as flat. This gives us the notion of real-time scaling information. Several recent writers have raised criticisms of my theory of the illusions, but there does not seem to be any strong evidence or arguments against it. (Some writers have omitted a vital point of the theory that typical depth-features, such as perspective, can set constancy scaling directly, even when depth is not seen. But without this direct setting of size scaling we cannot explain how a figure can be distorted though seen flat. I regard this direct setting of scale by typical features not as an *ad hoc* assumption – but as an example of applying scaling factors as in any indirect scientific measurement.) For other accounts of illusions, see Luckeisch (a useful and classic account, but no theory), Tolansky (no theory, but good examples, including the moon illusion in in art). For the history, see Boring, *Sensation and Perception in the history of experimental Psychology* (1942).

Size- and shape-constancy were clearly described in 1637, by Descartes in the *Dioptrics*. (The passage is quoted in my *Eye and Brain*, page 152.) The first experiments were by R.H.Thouless (1931, 1932) on what he called 'phenomenal regression to the real object'. See also E.Brunswick (1933, 1944) and K.Eissler

(1933) and W.H.Ittelson (1951). K.Koffka (1935) gives a theory in terms of perceived shape and distance (I believe this to be but half the story) and this is discussed by F.J.Langdon, with experiments (1951, 1953). For developmental studies see H.Leibowitz, *Visual Perception* (1965). For cross-cultural studies, especially with reference to the illusions, see M.H.Segall, D.T.Campbell and M.J.Herskovits, *The Influence of Culture on Visual Perception* (1966).

5 Scaling the universe

There is a surprisingly small literature on the philosophy of measurement, but see B.Ellis, *Basic Concepts of Measurement* (1968). The methods and the assumptions made by astronomers for measuring stellar distances are more or less explicitly described in many technical and more popular books on astronomy, for example *Larousse Encyclopedia of Astronomy* (1959).

How do we Scale the Moon and the Stars?
The apparent size of the moon has been measured with an optical comparison system in L.Kaufman and I.Rock, 'The moon illusion' (1962); and Tolansky (1964) has an interesting discussion of the size it is represented in paintings. It is likely that the reason why the Greeks considered the stars to lie at the same distance, fixed to a rotating celestial globe, was that they could not otherwise explain why the stars should move together, as they regarded the Earth as stationary. The planets ('wanderers'), and the sun and moon, were of course given their own crystal spheres.

6 Drawing in two-dimensional space

Examples of the curious perspective of primitive, classical and medieval drawing and painting will be found in any history of art. Gombrich came to feel that he underestimated the problem in his *Art and Illusion* (see Gombrich, 1965). There are many accounts of the Renaissance development of geometrical perspective, the principal work in the development of perspective drawing being J.White, *The Birth and Rebirth of Pictorial Space* (1958). I have tried to come to an independent assessment of a confused situation, finding Gombrich and White most useful; see also E.Short, *History of Religious Architecture* (1925, 4th ed. 1955). The quotation on Arnolfo di Cambio is from Short, page 250. The examples of Egyptian supposedly technical drawings are from H.S.Baker, *Furniture in the Ancient World* (1966). (This argument may be original and seems worth following up as a clue to ancient motives and capabilities. My position is not universally accepted by practising artists.) Examples of many viewpoints combined in Egyptian art will be found in any illustrated history, including Desroches-Noblecourt, *Tutankhamen* (1963). Technical drawings are more difficult to find, but there are technical papyri, especially medical.

For Canaletto's use of the *camera obscura* see W.G.Constable, *Canaletto* (1962).

7 Drawing in three-dimensional space

The stereoscope was first described by Sir Charles Wheatstone (1838). For information on photographic methods see L.P.Dudley (1951), R. & N. Spottiswoode (1953), and N.A.Valyus (1962). For the physiological basis, for corresponding contour theories and data, see K.Ogle, *Researches in Binocular Vision* (1950) and for the recent, important cross-correlation approach see B. Julesz (1960) and his later papers.

The first of the author's 3-D drawing machines was described briefly in 'Seeing in depth' (1965) but they have not yet been fully described, except for British Patent Application No. 12443/67.

8 Pictures, symbols and thought

The principal authority on the history of writing is David Diringer. See D.Diringer, *Writing* (1962) and *The Alphabet* (1968). The principal work on Egyptian language is Sir Alan Gardiner's *Egyptian Grammar* (1927, 3rd ed. 1957). For a complete Egyptian text with translation, see E.A.Wallis Budge, *The Egyptian Book of the Dead* (tr. 1895; Dover reprint 1967).

Recently J.H.Pullan in *The History of the Abacus* (1969) pointed out that the abacus has been used extensively since prehistoric times and that mechanical aids to calculation have almost always been employed. The early ways of writing numbers – cuneiform, Egyptian, hieroglyphic, Chinese, Phoenician, Mayan, Etruscan, Roman – all used scripts adapted to recording the number of tallies and the position of jetons on an abacus (Diringer, 1968). The very fact that such simple devices are so helpful is, surely, strong evidence that our brains do not work in this way. Hence my suggestion that symbols, language and counting methods allow us to use our brains in a non-biological way.

The intriguing thought that the neolithic monument Stonehenge on Salisbury Plain is a calculating engine for predicting eclipses, seasons and so on, comes from G.S.Hawkins, *Stonehenge Decoded* (1966) and has been taken seriously by the astronomer Fred Hoyle (1966). It is suggested that its great size was necessary to obtain the required permanence and accuracy of angular readings. It should be added that the biologist J.Z.Young previously suggested a very different reason: that the people could *get inside* their socially integrating symbol, before the invention of portable symbols such as written and printed letters in books (J.Z.Young, *Doubt and Certainty in Science* (1951)). Both could be correct.

Language

The philosophical mystery of language was explored by Descartes, whose views are coming back into prominence, and by Wittgenstein in his *Tractatus Logico-Philosophicus* (1922) where he discussed the structure of language and the structure of the world of facts. This is taken up again in *Philosophical Investigations* (1953) where the view is considerably different. In the *Investigations* there are also very interesting statements on perception.

I am all too conscious that the pioneer work of Jean Piaget is not explicitly discussed; but his influence must surely be evident. Of his many books, perhaps the most important in this connection are *The Language and Thought of the Child* (1926) and *The Origins of Intelligence in Children* (1952).

For a general discussion of the brain and language see E.H. Lenneberg (1964). The study on the brains and speaking ability of dwarfs is H.P.G.Seckel, *Birdheaded Dwarfs: studies in developmental anthropology including human proportions* (1960). Interesting anatomical differences between chimp and human brains, especially in the richness of association pathways, is given in N. Geschwind, 'The development of the brain and the evolution of language' (1964). A current experiment, too incomplete to assess, is that of J.R.Gardner on teaching the chimp Washoe deaf and dumb sign language, to establish whether the trouble is purely vocal, or conceptual. The standard general text on experiments on language, with an eye on informational problems, is G.A.Miller, *Language and Communication* (1951).

I have hardly touched upon the important work on linguistics associated with Noam Chomsky. Chomsky suggests that the human brain structures language according to innately given syntactical structural rules, from which sentences of various forms can be generated. This 'deep structure' underlying language is not itself language, but is regarded as innately given in the human, though not in other, brains. It is tempting for us to suppose that the deep structure of language is the expression of the much earlier 'perceptual hypotheses' used to order and predict the world of objects. If the structured perceptual hypotheses were taken over by the newly developed language, the difficulty of supposing that language deep structure could have developed by natural selection since the chimps largely disappears, for we may regard it as a 'take over' operation from what already existed in animal brains. Also, the close connection between how we see and how we think becomes less mysterious.

For this structural linguistics see N. Chomsky, *Syntactic Structures* (1957), Chomsky, 'The formal nature of language' (in Lenneberg, 1967) and J.Katz, *The Philosophy of Language* (1966). For more traditional background information, see P.Henle (ed.), *Language, Thought and Culture* (1966) and R.C.Oldfield and J.C.Marshall (eds.), *Language* (1968).

Since grammar is regarded as capable of generating sentences (and allowing us to understand an infinite number of sentences not previously heard or seen) it should be possible to represent and test it with an analytical computer programme in which acceptable sentence structures are generated by specific algorithms. This has been done by J.P.Thorne, P.Bratley and H. Dewer (1968). See also the work on introspective accounts of thinking and computer programming by A. Newell and H.A. Simon (1961).

For the role of induction and deduction, and the importance of hypotheses in formalised scientific thinking, see R.B.Braithwaite, *Scientific Explanation* (1949) and K.Popper, *The Logic of Scientific Discovery* (1959). It is interesting that recent philosophers of scientific method and many perceptual psychologists stress that the gaining of knowledge is more than a passive acquisition of facts, and also that it is not in essence a process which can be carried out by statable algorithms. We have no algorithms (sets of rules) for invention or discovery. See P.B. Medawar, *Induction and Intuition in Scientific Thought* (1969) and *The Art of the Soluble* (1967).

9 Seeing how things work

Seeing how things work appears to be, like language, virtually a uniquely human accomplishment. Even the simple putting together of two sticks, after contemplating the situation, by Köhler's chimp is regarded as exceptional.

Charles Babbage, the nineteenth-century mathematician and inventor of the modern computer, came to find working drawings inadequate and devised a special symbolism, somewhat like musical notation, for expressing the functional relations of the parts of machines. He used the works of a clock for demonstrating his language, relating its structure to function (see figure 135). See C.Babbage 'On a method of expressing by signs the action of machinery' (1826).

Bibliography

Adrian, Lord, *The Physical Background of Perception* (Waynflete Lectures 1946), London, 1947.

Adrian, Lord, *The Basis of Sensation: The Action of the Sense Organs*, London, 1949.

Arnheim, R. 'Gestalt and Art', *J. of Aesthetics and Art Criticism*, *2*, 71–5 (1943). Also in Hogg, J. (ed.), *Psychology of the Visual Arts*, Harmondsworth, 1969.

Arnheim, R. *Art and Visual Perception*, Berkeley, 1954.

Attneave, F. 'Some informational aspects of visual perception', *Psych. Review*, *61*, 183–198 (1954).

Babbage, C. 'On a method of expressing by signs the action of machinery', *Phil. trans. Roy. Soc.* (1826).

Baker, H.S. *Furniture in the Ancient World*, London, 1966.

Bartlett, F.C. *Remembering*, Cambridge, 1932.

Beardslee, D.C. & Wertheimer, M. (eds.), *Readings in Perception*, Princeton, 1958.

Benham, C.E. 'The artificial spectrum top', *Nature Lond. 51*, 200 (1894).

Berkeley, G. *A New Theory of Vision* (1709).

Boring, E.G. *Sensation and Perception in the History of Experimental Psychology*, New York, 1942.

Braithwaite, R.B. *Scientific Explanation*, London, 1949.

Brindley, G.S. *Physiology of the Retina and the Visual Pathway*, Monogr. of Physiol. Soc. 6, London, 1960.

Broadbent, D.E. *Perception and Communication*, Oxford, 1958.

Brown, J.L. 'Afterimages' in Graham, C.H. *Vision and Visual Perception*, pp. 479–503, New York, 1965.

Brown, J.L. 'Flicker and visual perception', in Graham, C.H. *Vision and Visual Perception*, New York, 1965.

Bruner, S.J. 'On perceptual readiness', *Psych. Rev. 64*, 123–52 (1957).

Bruner, S.J. *Studies in Cognitive Growth*, New York, 1966.

Brunswik, E. 'Die Zuganglichkeit von Gegenstanden fur Wahrnemungen und deren orientative Bestimmung', *Arch. ges. Psychol. 88*, 377–419 (1933).

Brunswik, E. 'Distal focusing of perception; size constancy in a representative sample of situations', *Psych. Monogr. 56*, 254 (1344).

Budge, E.A.Wallis, *The Egyptian Book of the Dead* (1895). Dover reprint, 1967.

Cherry, C. *On Human Communication*, New York, 2nd ed. 1966.

Chomsky, N. *Syntactic Structures*, The Hague, 1957.

Chomsky, N. 'The formal nature of language', in Lenneberg, E.H. *The Biological Foundations of Language*, New York, 1967.

Cohen, J.C. & Gordon, D.A. 'The Prévost-Fechner-Benham subjective colours', *Psych. Bull. 46*, 2, 97–136 (1949).

Constable, W.G. *Canaletto*, London, 1962.

Craik, K.J.W. *The Nature of Explanation*, Cambridge, 1943.

Descartes, R. *Philosophical Works*, ed. E.S.Haldane & G.R.T. Ross, London, 1967.

Descartes, R. *Dioptric*, Leyden, 1637. Also in *Philosophical Writings*, tr. N.K.Smith, London, 1952.

Desroches-Noblecourt, C. *Tutankhamen*, London, 1963.

Diringer, D. *Writing*, London, 1962.

Diringer, D. *The Alphabet: a Key to the History of Mankind*, London, 1968.

Dudley, L.P. *Stereoptics*, London, 1951.

Duke-Elder, W.S. *System of Ophthalmology*; Vol. I, *The Eye in Evolution*, London, 1958.

Eisler, K. 'Gestaltkonstanz der Sehdinge dei Variation der Objekte und ihre Einwirkungsweise auf den Wahrnemenden', *Arch. ges. Psychol. 88*, 487–551 (1933).

Ellis, W.H. (ed.), *Source Book of Gestalt Psychology*, London and New York, 1938.

Ellis, B. *Basic Concepts of Measurement*, London, 1958.

Evans, C. 'Some studies of pattern recognition using a stabilised image', *Brit. J. Psychol. 56*, 2 and 3, 121–33 (1965).

Evans, C. 'Further study of pattern perception and stabilised retinal images: the use of prolonged after images to achieve perfect stabilisation', *Brit. J. Psychol. 58*, 315–27 (1967).

Feigenbaum, E.A. & Feldman, J. *Computers and Thought*, London, 1963.

Fodor, J.A. & Katz, J. *The Structure of Language*, Englewood Cliffs, 1964.

Gardiner, A. *Egyptian Grammar* (1927), Oxford, 3rd ed. 1957.

Geschwind, N. *The Development of the Brain and the Evolution of Language*. Monogr. Series on Language and Linguistics No. 17. Report on the 15th Annual R.T.M. on Linguistic and Language Studies, 1964.

Gibson, J.J. *The Perception of the Visual World*, London and New York, 1950.

Gibson, J.J. *The Senses Considered as Perceptual Systems*, New York, 1966.

Gombrich, E.H. *Art and Illusion*, London, 1960.

Gombrich, E.H. 'Visual discovery through art', *Arts Magazine* (1965). Also in Hogg, J. (ed.), *Psychology and the Visual Arts*, Harmondsworth, 1969.

Graham, C.H. *Vision and Visual Perception*, New York, 1965.

Gregory, R.L. 'A technique for minimizing the effects of atmospheric disturbance on photographic telescopes', *Nature, Lond. 203*, 4942, 274–5 (1964).

Gregory, R.L., Wallace, J.G. & Campbell, F.W. 'Changes in size of visual after-images during changes of position in space', *Quart. J. Exp. Psychol. 11*, 1, 54–5 (1959).

Gregory, R.L., Anstis, S.M. & Shopland, C.D. 'Measuring visual constancy for stationary or moving objects', *Nature, Lond. 193*, 4815, 605–6 (1961).

Gregory, R.L. 'Distortion of visual space as inappropriate constancy scaling', *Nature, Lond. 119*, 678 (1963).

Gregory, R.L. & Shopland, C.D. 'The effect of touch on a visually ambiguous three-dimensional figure', *Quart. J. Exp. Psychol. 16*, 1 (1964).

Gregory, R.L. 'Stereoscopic Shadow-images', *Nature 203*, 1407–8 (1964).

Gregory, R.L. 'Will seeing machines have illusions?', *Machine Intelligence*, 1, Collins, N.L. & Michie, D. (eds.), Edinburgh and London, 1967.

Gregory, R.L. 'Seeing in depth', *Proc. Roy. Instn. 40*, 185 (1965).

Gregory, R.L. *Eye and Brain*, London, 1966.

Gregory, R.L. 'Origin of eyes and brains', *Nature, Lond. 213*, 5047, 369–72 (1967).

Gregory, R.L. 'Perceptual illusions and brain models', *Proc. Roy. Soc. 'B'* (1968).

Hawkins, G.S. *Stonehenge Decoded*, London, 1966.

Helmholtz, H. *Handbook of Physiological Optics*, Dover reprint, 1963.

Henle, P. (ed.), *Language, Thought and Culture*, Univ. Michigan Press/Ambassador, Canada (1958), Paperback 1965.

Hochberg, J.E. 'Effects of the Gestalt revolution', *Psych. Rev. 64*, 2, 16–19 (1957).

Hochberg, J.E. *Perception*, Englewood Cliffs, 1964.

Holland, H.C. *The Spiral After-Effect*, Oxford, 1965.

Holway, A.H. & Boring, E.G. 'Determinants of apparent visual size with distance variant', *Amer. J. Psychol. 54*, 21 (1941).

Hospers, J. *Meaning and Truth in the Arts*, Chapel Hill, N.C., 1946.

Hoyle, F. 'Speculations on Stonehenge', *Antiquity, 40*, 160, 262–76 (1966).

Hubel, D.H. & Wiesel, T.N. 'Receptive fields, binocular interaction and functional architecture in the cat's visual cortex', *J. Physiol. 160*, 106 (1962).

Hubel, D.H. & Wiesel, T.N. 'Receptive fields and functional architecture of monkey striate cortex', *J. Physiol. 195*, 215–43 (1968).

Ittelson, W.H. 'Size as a cue to distance', *Amer. J. Psychol. 64*, 54–67; 188–202 (1951).

Ittelson, W.H. *Visual Space Perception*, New York, 1960.

Ittelson, W.H. *The Ames Demonstrations in Perception*, London and Princeton, 1952, new ed. New York, 1968.

Julesz, B. 'Binocular depth perception of computer-generated patterns', *J. Bell Telephone Co. 39*, 1125 (1960).

Kaufman, L. & Rock, I. 'The moon illusion', *Sci. Amer. 204*, 120 (1962).

Katz, J.J. *The Philosophy of Language*, New York and London, 1966.

Köffka; K. *Principles of Gestalt Psychology*, New York, 1935.

Köhler, W. 'Physical Gestalten' (1920) in Ellis, W.H. (ed.), *Source Book of Gestalt Psychology*, London, 1938.

Köhler, W. *Dynamics of Psychology*, London and New York, 1940.

Krechesvsky, I. 'Brain Mechanisms and "Hypotheses"', *J. Comp. Psychol. 19*, 425–68, 1935.

Langdon, F.J. 'The perception of a changing shape', *Quart. J. Exp. Psychol. 3*, 157–65 (1951).

Langdon, F.J. 'Further studies in the perception of a changing shape', *Quart. J. Exp. Psychol. 5*, 89–107 (1953).

Larousse Encyclopedia of Astronomy, Eng. tr. London, 1959.

Lee, D. 'Theory of the stereoscopic shadow-caster, an instrument for the study of binocular kinetic space perception', *Vision Research 9*, 145–56 (1969).

Leibowitz, H. *Visual Perception*, New York, 1965.

Lenneberg, E.H. *The Biological Foundations of Language*, New York, 1967.

Lenneberg, E.H. *A Biological Perspective of Language. New Directions in the Study of Language*, Cambridge, Mass., 1964.

Lettvin, J.Y., Maturana, H.R., Pitts, W. & McCulloch, W.S. 'What the frog's eye tells the frog's brain', *Proc. Inst. Radio Engineers, N.Y. 47*, 1940 (1959).

Mach, E. *Space and Geometry in the Light of Physiological, Psychological and Physical Inquiry* (1906), tr. McCormack, T.J., Chicago, 1906.

Mach, E. *The Analysis of Sensations* (1886), Dover reprint, 1959.

Medawar, P.B. *The Art of the Soluble*, London, 1967.

Medawar, P.B. *Induction and Intuition in Scientific Thought,* London, 1969.

Miller, G.A. *Language and Communication,* London, 1951.

Miller, G.A. 'The magic number seven; plus or minus two; some limits to our capacity for processing information', *Psych. Rev. 63,* 81–97 (1956).

Morgan, W.D. & Lester, H. *Stereo Realist Manual,* New York, 1954.

Morris, D. *The Biology of Art,* London, 1962.

Morrison, P. & E. *Charles Babbage and his Calculating Engines,* Dover, 1961.

Müller-Lyer, F.C. 'Optische Urtheilstusehungen', *Arch. Physiol. Suppl.* Bd. 2, 263–70 (1889).

McCollough, C. 'Colour adaptation of edge detectors in the human visual system', *Science, 149,* 1115–16 (1965).

Nasmyth, J. See S. Smiles (ed.), *James Nasmyth Engineer: an Autobiography,* London, 1885.

Necker, L.A. 'Observations on some remarkable phenomena seen in Switzerland; and an optical phenomenon which occurs on viewing of a crystal or geometrical solid', *Phil. Mag.* (3 ser.) *1,* 329–37 (1832).

Neisser, U. *Cognitive Psychology,* New York, 1967.

Newell, A. & Simon, H.A. 'G.P.S., a programme that stimulates human thought', Lernende Autometen, Munich: R. Oldenberg, K.G. (1961), and in Feigenbaum, E.A. & Feldman, J. (eds.), *Computers and Thought,* London, 1963.

Ogle, K.N. *Researches in Binocular Vision,* London, 1950.

Oldfield, R.C. & Marshall, J.C. (eds.), *Language,* Harmondsworth, 1968.

Oldfield, R.C. & Zangwill, O.L. 'Head's concept of schema and its application in contemporary British psychology', *Brit. J. Psychol. 32,* 4, 267–86 (1942), and later parts.

Penrose, L.S. & R. 'Impossible objects: a special type of illusion', *Brit. J. Psychol. 49,* 31 (1958).

Piaget, J. *The Origins of Intelligence in Children,* New York, 1952.

Piaget, J. *The Language and Thought of the Child* (1926), tr. M. & R. Gabin, London, 1960.

Pierce, J.R. *Signals, Symbols and Noise,* London, 1962.

Popper, K.R. *The Logic of Scientific Discovery,* London, 1959.

Pritchard, R.M., Heron, W. & Hebb, D.O. 'Visual perception approached by the method of stabilised images', *Canadian J. Psychol. 14,* 67–77 (1960).

Pullan, J.M. *The History of the Abacus,* New York, 1969.

Rubin, E. *Synoplevede Figurer,* Copenhagen, 1915. Tr. in Beardslee, D.C. & Westheimer, M. *op. cit.*

Rushton, W.A.H. 'Visual Adaptation', the Ferrier Lecture 1962. *Proc. Roy. Soc.* 'B', *162,* 20–46 (1965).

Rushton, W.A.H. 'Bleached rhodopsin and visual adaptation', *J. Physiol. 181,* 645–55 (1965).

Russell, B. *History of Western Philosophy,* London, 1946.

Schiller, P. & Wiener, M. 'Binocular and Stereoscopic Viewing of Geometric Illusions', *Perceptual and Motor Skills, 15,* 739–47 (1962).

Seckel, H.P.G. *Birdheaded Dwarfs: studies in developmental anthropology including human proportions,* Springfield, Ill., 1960.

Segall, M.H., Campbell, D.T. & Herskovits, M.J. *The Influence of Culture on Visual Perception,* New York, 1966.

Shannon, C.E. & Weaver, W. *A Mathematical Theory of Communication,* Urbana, 1949.

Short, E. *A History of Religious Architecture* (1925), 4th ed. London, 1955.

Spottiswoode, R. & N. *The Theory of Stereoscopic Transmission and its Application to the Motion Picture*, Berkeley, 1953.

Tausch, R. 'Optische Tauschungen als artifizielle Effect der Gestaltungsprozess von Grossen und Formenkonstanz in der naturlichen Raunwahrnehmung', *Psychol. Forsch. 24*, 299–348 (1954).

Thiéry, A. 'Ueber geometrisch-optische Tauschungen', *Phil. Stud. 12*, 67–125 (1896).

Thorne, J.P. 'Grammars and Machines', *Trans. Phil. Soc.* 30–45 (1964).

Thorne, J.P., Bratley, P. & Dewer, H. 'The syntactical analysis of English by machine', in D. Michie (ed.), *Machine Intelligence, 3*, Edinburgh, 1968.

Thouless, R.H. 'Phenomenal Regression to the Real Object, 1', *Brit. J. Psychol. 21*, 339 (1931).

Thouless, R.H. 'Individual Differences in Phenomenal Regression', *Brit. J. Psychol. 22*, 216 (1932).

Tibbetts, P. (ed.), *Perception: Selected Readings in Science and Phenomenology*, Chicago, 1969.

Tolansky, S. *Optical Illusions*, Oxford, 1964.

Valyus, N.A. *Stereoscopy*, London and New York, 1962.

Vernon, M.D. 'The functions of schemata in perceiving', *Psych. Rev. 62*, 180–92 (1955).

Walls, G.L. *The Vertebrate Eye and its Adaptive Radiation*, Cranbrook Institute Science Bull. 19 (1942).

Wertheimer, M. *Principles of Perceptual Organisation* (1923), tr. in Ellis, W.H. *Source Book of Gestalt Psychology*, London and New York, 1938.

Wheatstone, C. 'On some remarkable, and hitherto unobserved phenomena of binocular vision', *Phil. trans. Roy. Soc. 128* (1838).

White, J. *The Birth and Rebirth of Pictorial Space*, London, 1958.

Wittgenstein, L. *Tractatus Logico-Philosophicus*, London, 1922.

Wittgenstein, L. *Philosophical Investigations*, tr. Anscombe, G.E.M., Oxford, 1953.

Wollheim, R. 'Art and Illusion', *Brit. J. Aesthet. 3*, 15–37 (1963).

Wohlmgemuth, A. *On the After-Effect of Seen Movement*, Brit. J. Psychol. Monogr. 1 (1911).

Young, J.Z. *Doubt and Certainty in Science*, London, 1951.

Zweigler, H.P. & Leibowitz, H.W. 'Apparent visual size as a function of distance for children and adults', *Amer. J. Psychol. 70*, 1, 106–109.

Index